FEMI
The Diary of a Yoruba Demon

Femi Alashi

This is based on a true life story.

Prologue

Their loves, their hates, their passions, all died with them. They will never again take part in anything that happens in this world.

Go ahead — eat your food and be happy; drink your wine and be cheerful. It's all right with God.

Always look happy and cheerful.

Enjoy life with the woman you love, as long as you live the ~~useless~~ life that God has given you in this world. Enjoy every ~~useless~~ day of it, because that is all you will get for all your trouble.

Chapter One

"A Birthday to Remember"

I remember it clearly now, every detail, pixel, frame, and second. I was living in the moment, with nothing to worry about as I reclined on the sun-warmed deck of the luxury yacht, my legs casually dangling over the edge. My feet skimmed the clear, light-blue waters of Saint Tropez, creating ripples that glinted under the golden hues of the setting sun. The sky above transformed into a canvas of orange and pink, casting a warm glow that embraced the beach and the swaying palm trees along the shore. The rhythmic sound of waves crashing against the sand and the distant laughter from the beachgoers filled the air, blending with the soft strains of Afrobeat music from the yacht's speakers.

Below me, the crystalline water revealed a lively underwater world, with schools of colorful fish darting back and forth. I breathed in the salty air, a mix of sea breeze and a hint of grilled seafood from a nearby beachside cafe. I leaned back, laid on the towel on the yacht, my head on my hands, my eyes closed, as I absorbed the serene atmosphere. It was my twenty-seventh birthday, and I had invited my closest friends to celebrate in the idyllic setting of Saint Tropez, a far cry from my humble beginnings.

Once an introverted, bookish teenager back in Nigeria, I had transformed into a confident, charismatic young tech mogul. My journey from a small bedroom in Lagos to the heart of Silicon Valley was a tale of grit, ambition, and sheer brilliance. Started from nothing, I had built a multimillion-dollar tech empire that was the envy of many.

Opening my eyes, my gaze swept across the breathtaking panorama, but my mind was elsewhere. I had found myself reminiscing about simpler times, times when my burgeoning tech start-up was just a collection of ideas and late-night coding sessions. I remembered Moji, my best friend from those days, her laughter echoing in my memories. I had a crush on her, we both did on each other. We had shared dreams and aspirations under the starlit Lagos sky, and I had been her confidant, her shoulder to cry on when things went south with her then-boyfriend, Kunle. Things were really simple then but as my company grew, so did the distance between Moji and I.

I became consumed by my work, slowly drifting away from Moji, caught up in a whirlwind of success and recognition. I often regretted how I had let our friendship fade, a casualty of my ambition.

Lost in my thoughts, I barely registered the hand on my shoulder that snapped me back to reality. "You okay, man?" asked Zeke, a college friend and now a key member of my executive team, as he settled beside me.

I managed a half-smile. "Yeah, just lost in the past for a moment."

"Thinking about Moji?" Zeke's voice was gentle, and understanding.

I took a deep breath, a tinge of regret in my voice. "Yeah. I saw her wedding pictures with Kunle on social media. It's... surreal."

Zeke nodded, his eyes reflecting a mix of sympathy and pragmatism. "I get it, bro. But you've got to focus on the here and now. Look at all this," he gestured expansively, "your success, your friends. We're here to celebrate you, man."

Zeke's eyes sparkled with mischief as he nudged me playfully. "Speaking of celebration, did you see Maria in that stunning orange bikini?"

I was caught off guard, turned towards him. "Maria? I haven't really been..."

"Trust me, she's been looking for you. That bikini is definitely making a statement," Zeke remarked with a grin.

I shook my head, trying to clear the cobwebs of nostalgia. Zeke was right. It was time to let go of the past and embrace the present and look forward to the future. "You're right. Let's head back to the party."

As we walked back, Maria approached us with a bounce in her step. "There you are, Femi! We've been waiting for you to get things started!" Her voice was playful, her eyes sparkling with excitement.

I forced a smile, my mood gradually shifting. "Just needed a moment to enjoy the view."

Maria's gaze followed mine, taking in the stunning scenery. "It's beautiful, but I think the view here is even better," she said teasingly, her hand lightly touching my arm.

I chuckled, her flirtatious energy was infectious. "Well, I'm here now. Let's get this party started."

Maria beamed, her enthusiasm contagious. "Alright, everyone, gather around! I want to make a toast to our birthday boy." The guests turned their attention to her as she raised her glass. "To Femi, an extraordinary man, a visionary in business, and a dear friend. May this year bring you more success, joy, and maybe even a little romance," she added with a suggestive smile, her eyes locked on his.

The guests cheered, and I raised my glass with everyone, my heart lightening. Maria did that with a toast. Maybe it was time to start looking forward instead of back.

I felt a warmth in my cheeks, a blend of gratitude and a touch of embarrassment. I raised his glass in a smooth motion, my voice sure with sincerity, "Thank you, Maria. Having you all here means a lot to me."

Zeke, ever the vibrant spirit, chimed in with his glass held high, "To Femi, the man of the hour! And to the rest of us, lucky enough to bask in the glow of his success!"

Laughter rippled through the group as glasses clinked in unison. The mood was infectious, yet I found my thoughts drifting back to Moji and Kunle. A twinge of regret for what might have been with Moji lingered in my heart, a question of 'what if' that I couldn't quite shake off, so I downed my drink.

As the yacht swayed gently, the ambiance was filled with the upbeat rhythms of Afrobeats, setting the perfect tone for the evening. The aroma of French cuisine, notably the freshly grilled fish sourced just a short while ago, wafted enticingly through the air.

Maria, with a tray of colorful drinks, returned to my side. I was feeling slightly tipsy, but it was a pleasant buzz, enhancing the joyous atmosphere. Everyone was engrossed in conversation, laughter punctuating the air amidst the breathtaking backdrop of Saint Tropez.

She handed me a shot glass, and leaned in close, her voice a seductive whisper, "Celebrate with me, Femi. It's your day, after all."

I was caught in the allure of the moment, our glass clinked and we both downed the shot. The liquor's warmth spread through me, a fitting complement to the thrill of the evening.

Maria's laugh was light and infectious. "You're quite charming when you're tipsy," she said, her face inches from his, an unspoken invitation in her eyes. "I have a toast, just for you. Are you ready?"

Intrigued, I nodded, my pulse quickening in anticipation.

Maria's tone softened, her words intimate and heartfelt. "To you, Femi," she began, her eyes not leaving mine. "The man who captures hearts without trying. You're not just handsome and smart; you have a presence that's impossible to ignore."

I listened, Maria's words weaving a spell around me. I had always been drawn to her, but hearing her emotions laid bare was unexpected and exhilarating.

Maria continued, her voice earnest. "I want to be more than just another face in your crowd, Femi. I want us to explore what could be between us." Her gaze was steady, seeking an answer in my eyes.

My mind was racing, I paused, speechless for some seconds. The attraction was undeniable, the pull strong. I reached for her hand, my voice steady yet soft. "Maria, you're remarkable. I'm drawn to you in ways I didn't anticipate. Let's see where this journey takes us."

Maria's response was a smile that lit up her face. She moved closer, and our lips met in a kiss that was gentle yet spoke volumes. It was a moment of new beginnings, the promise of something yet to be explored.

We retreated to a more private corner of the yacht, the party continued, the music and laughter a vibrant backdrop to our growing connection. Inside the room, the world faded away, leaving only Maria and I, wrapped in the discovery of each other.

Outside, the party carried on, the guests oblivious to the intensity unfolding in privacy. Chidi, seated near the door, raised an eyebrow and grinned, his comment light-hearted, "Femi's having quite the birthday celebration, isn't he?"

In the secluded space, Maria and I were lost in the moment, a connection that was intense yet understood to be a fleeting escape. Our encounter was a celebration of the present, a mutual understanding of the joy in spontaneity.

Afterward, Maria looked up at me with a playful glint in her eyes. "Happy birthday," she whispered, her voice a mix of affection and mischief. "This was a celebration to remember."

I drew her in for another kiss as the sound of her last word hit the airwave. "Absolutely," I agreed, my mind clear of past regrets. I was content to enjoy the present, savoring the unexpected turn my birthday had taken.

***

Zeke turned to Khadi, his eyes twinkling with playful intent. "Khadi, be my partner in crime tonight. It's Femi's birthday, after all. Let's make it memorable," he suggested with a wink.

Khadi, unfazed, laughed and shook her head. "Zeke, your charm might work on others, but I'm immune," she replied, her tone light yet firm, taking a casual sip of her drink.

Undeterred, Zeke grinned. "Well, no harm in trying, right?" he said with a good-natured chuckle.

In the meantime, Maria and I reappeared, slightly unkempt but visibly relaxed. We joined our friends, they were gathered around Cody, busy pouring shots.

"To Femi, and to a birthday we'll never forget!" Cody raised his glass with enthusiasm.

The group echoed his cheer, the sound of their glasses clinking together filling the air. My face was filled with a genuine smile, a reflection of my appreciation for these moments with friends.

As the group enjoyed their shots, I noticed Louisa looking somewhat unsettled. She stood and gestured discreetly for me to follow. "Femi, can we talk?" she asked, her voice laced with a mix of nostalgia and tension.

Curious, I followed her to a quieter spot. "What's on your mind, Louisa?" I inquired, my tone gentle.

Louisa hesitated, searching for the right words. "Seeing you here, being around you... it stirs up a lot of old feelings. I care about you, Femi, but I know we're past what we had. It's just hard, you know?"

My curiosity softened in understanding. "I know, Louisa. It's not easy for me either. But I value our friendship too much to let it get awkward. We can navigate this together, as friends," I reassured her, my hand offering a comforting touch on her shoulder.

Louisa met my gaze with a hint of relief in her eyes. "Thank you, Femi. I didn't want to make things weird. Oh, and I have a birthday gift for you. I'll bring it to your room later," she said, a faint smile gracing her lips before she rejoined the others.

Watching her walk away, I felt a bittersweet ache. My feelings for Louisa lingered, yet I also knew our path lay in friendship, not romance. There was a reason we didn't work.

As the evening unfolded, the yacht brimmed with energy and laughter. I spent time catching up with Louisa, our interactions were easy yet tinged with a shared history. From a distance, Maria's gaze lingered on us, a flash of jealousy in her eyes despite the casual nature of her relationship with me.

Zeke, probably noticed Maria's fixed stare, approached her and tapped her shoulder lightly. "Hey, don't let jealousy cloud the night. Remember our strategy with Femi," he reminded her quietly.

Taking a deep breath, Maria nodded, regaining her composure. "You're right, Zeke. I can't let emotions get in the way of our plan. Thanks," she said, a renewed focus settling in her eyes.

Zeke offered a reassuring smile. "Just enjoy the night. And remember, we've got a goal in mind," he added, patting her back lightly.

Maria's expression brightened as she turned her attention back to the group, specifically to Femi, who was now engaged in conversation with Chidi.

Chidi, beaming with pride and nostalgia, clapped Femi on the back. "Bro, this is incredible. Remember how we used to dream of days like these back in Lagos? And here we are, living it," he exclaimed, his voice rich with emotion.

Femi's laughter mingled with Chidi's enthusiasm. "Those dreams are now our reality, man. It's surreal," he agreed, his eyes reflecting the joy of the moment.

Chidi, always the inquisitive one, leaned in with a sly grin. "By the way, Femi, is Khadi single?"

I raised an eyebrow at Chidi's question. "Why the sudden interest?"

Chidi flashed a mischievous grin. "She's stunning, isn't she? I'm thinking of making a move."

"Well, you'll have to find that out for yourself." I chuckled.

With a nod, Chidi approached Khadi confidently. "Enjoying the party?" he asked with a charming smile.

Khadi's response was warm. "Absolutely, it's fantastic."

Chidi leaned in, a hint of playfulness in his voice. "Just curious, are you single?"

A soft blush tinted Khadi's cheeks. "Yes, I am."

"Interesting," Chidi replied, his smile widening before he excused himself.

As the evening unwound, Chidi, ever the initiator, suggested they head back to the mansion and then out to Club Kiss. Passing by Khadi, he couldn't resist saying, "Looking forward to a dance with you later." His words left her with a shy smile, and the group buzzed with excitement about the night ahead.

At the mansion, everyone dispersed to their respective rooms to prepare for the club. The mansion's grandeur was evident in its high ceilings and opulent decor, each bedroom a luxurious sanctuary with stunning views.

Walking to their rooms, Maria teased Khadi about Chidi's evident interest. "Looks like someone caught Chidi's eye," she said playfully.

Khadi smiled, appreciative of Maria's light-heartedness. "Thanks, Maria. Let's see how the night unfolds. But what about you and Femi? There seemed to be quite a spark."

Maria's eyes gleamed with a mix of excitement and apprehension. "Femi and I had a moment, for sure. I'm really into him, just hoping it's mutual."

Khadi offered reassurance. "From what I could see, the interest is there. Just go with the flow."

"Appreciate it, Khadi," Maria replied as they reached their rooms.

Inside her room, Maria felt a twinge of jealousy at the thought of Louisa and Femi. Her focus on Femi was clear, yet she couldn't shake off the feeling that Louisa might become a distraction.

Khadi, meanwhile, reflected on Chidi's flirtation. She found him attractive but was hesitant to pursue anything. Enjoying her single status, she didn't want to complicate things.

As she prepared for the club, Khadi felt a mix of excitement and apprehension about the attention from Chidi. The night held endless possibilities.

Maria, determined to catch Femi's eye, chose a striking red dress that accentuated her figure. Her makeup was meticulously applied, enhancing her sultry gaze and full lips. Thoughts of Femi lingered as she readied herself.

As the man of the hour, I emerged looking sharp in a tailored black suit, complementing his athletic build. My hair, styled perfectly, and the sheen of my black leather shoes, added to his sophisticated aura.

Zeke's outfit, a fitted black shirt paired with jeans, was effortlessly stylish. The geometric pattern on his shirt and the sleekness of his leather boots added a contemporary edge, showcasing his robust physique.

Chidi, opting for a casual yet eye-catching style, wore a fitted white t-shirt adorned with an artistic graphic print, accentuating his muscular arms. He paired it with slim-fitting ripped jeans and white sneakers. His short hair was styled in a relaxed, wavy manner, adding to his effortlessly cool vibe.

Cody, the group's skilled mixologist, chose a smart-casual ensemble. He donned a fitted gray blazer over a crisp white dress shirt, matched with sleek black trousers. Black dress shoes and a tasteful silver watch completed his polished look, and his hair was neatly combed, reflecting his meticulous attention to detail.

In the living room, the group eagerly anticipated Khadi and Louisa's arrival. I caught sight of Maria in her stunning red dress, complimented her with a warm smile, "You look absolutely breathtaking, Maria."

Maria's cheeks tinted with a blush as she responded with a smile. "Thanks, Femi. You're quite the sight yourself," she teased with a playful wink.

Cody, overhearing the exchange, joined in with a chuckle. "Don't leave me out of the compliments, Femi," he joked, nudging my arm lightly. "But seriously, everyone's looking sharp tonight."

Zeke, glancing up from his phone, chimed in with a nod. "Definitely. Cody, that jacket is a standout choice."

Cody beamed, appreciative of the compliment. "Knew it was perfect for tonight."

Banter filled the room with a light-hearted energy as we anticipated the night ahead.

Khadi and Louisa soon made their grand entrance, turning heads with their striking club attire. Khadi's black dress hugged her curves, shimmering subtly, while Louisa's bold leather skirt and crop top combination exuded confidence. Chidi's gaze lingered on Khadi, his admiration evident in his compliments, causing her to smile bashfully.

The group departed for Club Kiss, their excitement palpable as they approached the vibrant venue. The club's entrance was alive with energy, the bouncers recognizing the group and granting them immediate entry.

Inside, the VIP section awaited them, bottles of champagne chilling in ice. The group raised their glasses in a toast to my birthday, the club's pulsating music and dynamic atmosphere enveloped us.

Chidi and Khadi found rhythm together on the dance floor, moving in sync to the music. I was watching them, soon after I leaned towards Maria and reiterated my admiration. "You really do look stunning tonight."

Maria's response was laced with a hint of playfulness. "You mentioned that already, Femi."

"Well, it bears repeating. You're beautiful." My chuckle was light.

Our conversation lingered in the air, filled with flirtation, unspoken questions and possibilities.

Louisa, meanwhile, mingled with familiar faces, and Zeke and Cody ventured onto the dance floor, returning with a group of captivating women. One of them caught my attention, her smile an open invitation. It was lust at first sight, somehow we both knew we needed each other's touch and companion that night. Maria watched, a knot of jealousy forming as she observed my interaction with this young lady whose beauty and smile got me captivated.

Zeke, noticing her discomfort, guided her aside. "Stay focused, Maria. Remember what we're here for. Let Femi enjoy his night."

Maria, grappling with her emotions, nodded reluctantly. She watched as Femi and the woman moved towards the club's exit, Zeke giving her a subtle nod. "Time to follow them," he urged.

With a deep breath, Maria steeled herself, she downed
her drink, her focus realigning with their initial plan,
even as her feelings remained in turmoil.

Outside, the cool night breeze was a welcome
contrast to the club's heated atmosphere. I introduced
the woman as Tessa, and the group exchanged
light-hearted banter. Maria struggled to maintain her
composure as Tessa's flirtations with me became
increasingly evident. Back at the mansion, gathered
around the shimmering pool, glasses of champagne in
hand, the group's laughter and conversations filled the
night.

Maria found herself fixated on me and Tessa, our
rapport growing visibly stronger. In a bid to bolster
her resolve, she downed a couple of shots of tequila,
feeling the fiery liquid embolden her spirit.

As the night deepened, Tessa leaned in to whisper to
me, I don't remember what she said to me but I had a
huge smile on my face, I couldn't hide it. This sparked
a rush of anticipation in Maria's heart. I had a hint of
mischief in my eyes, as I led Tessa towards my
bedroom. I caught Maria's gaze, and asked her with a
teasing look, "Want to join us?"

Maria hesitated, her emotions a tumultuous mix of
desire and apprehension. With a small nod, she

masked her uncertainty with a semblance of a smile, determined to see this through.

What followed was a night where passion supremely reigned, blurring lines and deepening connections. Maria found herself increasingly captivated by our shared intimacy forging a bond she hadn't anticipated.

As dawn crept in, casting a soft glow over the room, Maria lay there, entwined with me, her mind a whirl of emotions with Tessa on the other side of the bed. The night's events had brought us closer, yet she was acutely aware of the complexities that lay ahead. She snuggled closer to me, a mix of satisfaction and contemplation enveloping her.

With the morning sun rising, Maria knew our journey had just begun, a path laden with intrigue and passion, promising to shape their future in unforeseen ways.

Chapter Two

Louisa, returned to the mansion as the sun began to rise, she found herself captivated by the serene beauty of the sunrise. It was a moment of tranquility amidst the whirlwind of the night's events.

Louisa and I met in one of the classes, I noticed her in class, she looked exotic, a mix of what a goddess would be made of, if I had to create one myself. She challenged the professor teaching our class one day and that was when I realized she was not American, she had moved from France to study in the United States. Her accent was very obvious in every word she spoke, her intelligence got me hooked, I had to speak to her after class.

"You now have a target on your back for what you just did, you know," I said with a smile, hoping for a response that felt like it took hours to come.

"For providing my view on a topic, I know very well, I don't think so." She said with a smile. She raised her head and our gaze met. Her confidence got me hooked.

"I guess I have two professors for this course, you and Professor Lawrence." I said as she laughed.

My name is Femi, I'm Louisa. We shook hands, walked with her till I had to take another route for my next class, we exchanged numbers and spoke everyday from then on, became friends, and started dating till we ended our relationship.

I woke up amidst the soft breathing of Maria and Tessa. A content smile played on my lips as I remembered the night's escapades. The women were deep in slumber, and I chuckled softly, appreciating the shared memories.

My thoughts soon turned to Maria. Despite the complexities of the night, I couldn't ignore the growing connection I felt with her. I knew a conversation was needed to navigate our evolving relationship.

I woke them up with kisses, started with Maria because I could tell she was kinda awake followed by Tessa.

"Hey lovely," Tessa said as she tried to open her eyes. She got up from the bed, her butt cheeks clapping at intervals as she made her way to the bathroom while Maria lay there sleeping.

Downstairs, I joined Zeke and Cody, who were already deep in discussion over morning coffee. Louisa, rejuvenated from her night, joined them, her energy infectious while sharing little information on why she was just returning to the mansion this morning. As Maria and Tessa eventually made their appearance, Femi seized the opportunity to speak privately with Maria on the balcony.

In our intimate conversation, I expressed my growing feelings for Maria, candidly sharing my uncertainties and about the dynamics with Tessa and Louisa. It was a pivotal moment, one that deepened our understanding and connection. Maria felt like home with drops of naughtiness, I wanted that for myself.

As we rejoined the group, Zeke and Maria exchanged subtle glances, acknowledging the progression of their plan. After Tessa and her friends departed, Zeke unveiled the next surprise, a private wine-tasting event, followed by dinner at an exquisite French restaurant along the coast.

With the day's plans set, the group dispersed to prepare. Maria, in the solitude of her shower, reflected on the complexities and exhilaration of the situation, gearing up for the adventures yet to come.

Adorned in a floral dress paired with strappy sandals, Maria joined the group aboard the yacht, basking in the warm sunlight as they cruised along the coast. Upon reaching the vineyard, they were warmly greeted by the owner, who offered a tour and shared the rich history of the estate. The wine tasting was a sensory delight, with each variety offering a unique taste, complemented by the stunning vistas of the vineyard.

After the vineyard visit, the group re-embarked on the yacht, their palates still tingling from the wine. They bought bottles of their favorite rosé and champagne. The anticipation for the birthday dinner at the exclusive French restaurant heightened as they neared their destination.

Arriving at the private dock of the restaurant, they were greeted by a friendly hostess, who couldn't help but give Femi an extra moment of attention.

"Party of Femi Williams," Zeke announced with a charming grin.

"Right this way, Mr. Williams," the hostess said, guiding them to a beautifully set table with an ocean view.

The restaurant exudes elegance, its warm ambiance complementing the soothing sounds of the sea. The group settled in, their senses enveloped by the aroma of gourmet cuisine.

Meanwhile, at the reception, a curious conversation unfolded between Reine, the hostess, and Elyna, one of the servers.

"What was that about?" Reine inquired, puzzled by Elyna's reaction.

Elyna, with a hint of surprise, asked, "You don't know who he is?"

"Should I?" Reine responded, intrigued.

Elyna quickly pulled out her phone, revealing a viral social media post of Femi. "That's Femi Williams," she said, her tone a mix of excitement and disbelief.

Reine's eyes widened in recognition. The man she had just greeted was none other than the celebrated Femi Williams, known for more than just his business acumen. Watching him interact with his friends, she felt a newfound admiration.

"He's even more impressive in person," Reine remarked, her gaze returning to Femi's table.

Elyna chuckled, her eyes playful. "And surrounded by such an attractive group. He's quite the catch."

Their conversation was a blend of awe and lighthearted speculation, reflecting the charisma and intrigue Femi carried with him.

Elyna, with a blend of confidence and charm, approached Femi's table. Back at the greeter's station, Reine watched with a mixture of admiration and curiosity.

"Good afternoon, everyone. I'm Elyna, and I'll be serving you today. Happy birthday, Mr. Williams!" she greeted, her smile bright and engaging.

The group responded warmly, clearly taken by Elyna's charismatic presence.

"Shall we start with some cocktails or would you prefer to go straight to your main drink orders?" Elyna inquired, her attention flitting between me and my friends.

Just as I was about to answer, my phone rang, interrupting the moment. "Excuse me, I need to take this," I said, stepping away from the table.

As I walked off, answering the call, my face lit up. "Hello, Mom."

My mother's voice, filled with affection and pride, came through. "Happy birthday, my dear boy!"

I was touched by genuine warmth. "Thank you, Mom."

My mother's blessings flowed over the phone, her words echoing the depth of her love. "Your father wants to speak with you," she added.

I was surprised at my father's eagerness to join in, it became evident when I responded. "Really, Dad?"

Our conversation was light-hearted, I laughed mingling at my father's curious inquiries about the party.

Meanwhile, Elyna observed Femi from a distance. His easygoing charm and genuine warmth were impossible to ignore. She made a mental note to engage him more personally.

Returning from my call, I approached Elyna. "Sorry about that," I said, my voice smooth. "So, what do you recommend for a drink?"

Elyna's cheeks flushed with a subtle smile. "I'm glad you asked, Mr. Williams. Our menu has a wide selection, but for you, everything is on the menu."

My eyes twinkled mischievously, leaned in slightly. "In
that case, I'm curious about the best champagne
France has got to offer with its sweetest dessert."

Elyna's playful response was accompanied by a coy
look, adding a hint of flirtation to the air.

As I rejoined my friends at the table, Zeke was
pouring a round of champagne. Handing me a glass,
Zeke raised an eyebrow inquisitively.

"Just catching up with my parents," I explained,
settling into my seat.

The group then lifted their glasses in a toast to me,
celebrating the occasion with a cheer and the
anticipation of an unforgettable evening ahead.

Elyna returned to the table, gracefully balancing a
bottle of champagne in her arm. As she set it before
me with a flair, her elegant smile and attire caught my
eye. "A special gift for your birthday, compliments of
our restaurant, the best champagne from France" she
announced.

The group expressed their awe and appreciation.
Cody murmured, "Wow," visibly impressed by the
gesture.

"Thank you," I replied, offering Elyna a warm, appreciative smile.

"Are you ready to order your meals?" Elyna asked, her tone professional yet friendly.

After a quick consultation around the table, I conveyed everyone's readiness. Elyna attentively noted each person's order, then turned back to me with a polite smile.

"And for you, sir? What would you like this evening?" she inquired.

I ordered a selection of appetizers for the table, including prawns, calamari, and zucchini. For his main course, I chose the Tropez steak. Upon Elyna's query about my preference, I specified, "Medium rare, leaning towards rare, please."

Zeke watched the interaction with an amused expression, noting the brief yet polite exchange between Elyna and I.

Elyna soon returned with the appetizers, each dish exquisitely presented, a testament to the restaurant's culinary expertise. The group indulged in the delicious starters, the table buzzing with lively conversations and laughter.

"Your steak will be out shortly," Elyna informed me, her professional demeanor unwavering. "Is there anything else I can assist you with for now?"

The group continued to enjoy their appetizers, the evening unfolding with a blend of good food, great company, and a celebratory atmosphere.

I smiled and asked, "No, thank you. Could you direct me to the restroom, please?"

"Of course, it's in the back," Maria interjected.

Elyna confirmed Maria's directions and escorted me to the restrooms.

"Which one is the men's room?" I inquired.

Elyna indicated the correct door, and I gently took her hand, guiding her into the restroom with me. She followed as I slightly pulled her in, "I want that French dessert, the sweetest one" I said as the door closed behind us, we shared a heated, forbidden moment. Locked in a passionate embrace, we quickly succumbed to our desires.

I had to cover her mouth with my hand, and would later put two fingers in her mouth to keep her quiet as I continued to thrust her. Elyna moaned quietly and she gently found her way to the wash-basin for support, the slippery wall failed us as we both reached the pinnacle of pleasure within minutes.

Upon exiting the restroom, I made sure no one saw Elyna leaving the restroom with me. I rejoined my friends at the table just minutes after my clandestine encounter with my steak waiting for me.

Twenty minutes later, Elyna and other staff members arrived with a birthday cake, lit with a single candle. They sang "Happy Birthday" to me, I was visibly touched by the gesture. The group captured the moment on their phones, adding to the evening's collection of memories.

I made a wish and blew out the candle, my friends cheered. The cake was distributed, and the group relished the sweet end to our meal.

As the evening began to wind down, Reine, the hostess, approached Femi. "Thank you for choosing our restaurant for your celebration, Mr. Williams. I hope you've enjoyed your birthday dinner."

I responded graciously, "It was fantastic, thank you. Everything was perfect."

Elyna, observing from a distance, smiled softly, content with having contributed to my special night.

The group then prepared to leave, I took a moment to thank the staff personally for their exceptional service. I also shared a brief, friendly exchange with Elyna, expressing my appreciation for her attentiveness and our encounter.

Back on the yacht, the atmosphere was relaxed and cheerful. The group decided to spend the remainder of the evening by the pool, enjoying the serene Saint Tropez night.

As they lounged by the water, conversation flowed freely. Chidi, looking thoughtful, suddenly confessed, "I really think I might have found someone special."

The group erupted in light-hearted teasing, but Chidi's sincerity was evident.

As the evening unfolded by the pool, I glanced around and queried, "Where are the ladies? They've been gone for quite some time."

Louisa, emerging in a flowing sundress over her bikini, responded with a playful apology, "Sorry to keep you waiting. Khadi and Maria are still getting ready."

The group welcomed Louisa with light-hearted compliments and chuckles as she elegantly dove into the pool. Zeke, seizing the moment, joked about fetching more champagne and playfully teased me about opting for water instead.

Shortly after, Khadi appeared, her presence commanding attention in a stunning yellow swimsuit. As she walked past, Zeke commented with a friendly grin, "Chidi's in for a treat tonight."

Khadi, smiling, replied, "Let's see if he thinks so."

Zeke ascended the stairs, his gaze locked on Maria's room at the end of the hallway. Upon reaching her door, he inhaled deeply and entered without knocking.

Maria, standing in front of her mirror and adjusting her bikini top, was startled by the sudden intrusion. She whipped around, her eyes wide with shock as she registered Zeke's presence in her room. Her heart pounded in her chest, and she crossed her arms over herself defensively. She managed a strained smile, struggling to mask her unease. "Hey, Zeke," she said, aiming to be casual.

"Hey, beautiful," Zeke responded, appraising Maria's figure with a predatory gaze.

Maria squirmed under his scrutiny, aware of his infatuation but uninterested in reciprocation. Hoping to deflect, she asked, "Is everything okay, Zeke?"

"Everything's perfect now that I'm with you," he said suggestively, inching closer.

Maria's heart raced, her instincts urging her to escape the escalating situation. "Zeke, I think you should leave before someone catches us," she said calmly.

Disappointment flickered across Zeke's face, but he knew she was right. As his lust burned, he issued a demand. "I need to have some time with you before you get pregnant for Femi," he said.

"Pregnant? That wasn't part of the plan," Maria objected.

"It is now. A man like Femi won't fall in love easily; it takes a combination of factors. Don't forget who you're dealing with. You wouldn't want me to use the video I have of you. We'll talk more when we get back to California," Zeke said, turning towards the door.

Relief washed over Maria as he left. She took a deep breath, steadying her pounding heart.

Unbeknownst to them, Cody had observed Zeke's exit from Maria's room, suspicion igniting his curiosity. He couldn't help but wonder what had transpired behind the closed door, and whether Maria was alright. He decided to keep an eye on Zeke, in case his intentions proved harmful. With these thoughts in mind, he kept his concerns to himself for the time being, and continued to the bathroom, contemplating whether or not to share his observations with me.

***

"There he is," the group chorused as Zeke returned, arms laden with champagne bottles.

Moments later, Maria appeared in a striking red bikini and settled beside me. We lounged poolside, sipping drinks and engaging in lively conversation. I couldn't help but notice Chidi and Khadi's absence. "Hey, have you seen Chidi and Khadi?" I inquired.

Maria cast a sly smile. "Oh, I think they're preoccupied with each other," she said, gesturing towards the cabana.

I glimpsed Chidi and Khadi locked in a passionate embrace and grinned, I was pleased for my friend. The group spent the remainder of the night playing games and reveling in each other's company.

The evening by the pool was a blend of joy and ease, the group's laughter and conversations echoing into the night. However, as the party wound down and everyone retired to their rooms, Maria found herself alone with her thoughts, which were heavy and conflicted.

The memory of Zeke's earlier intrusion lingered in her mind, casting a shadow over the night's merriment. She felt unsettled by his advances, which had strayed far from their friendly dynamics. The situation had brought an unexpected complication to the plan she and Zeke had originally crafted to win my affections.

Maria sat on her bed, wrestling with her emotions. Her growing feelings for me, which had started as part of their scheme, had started to evolve into something more genuine. This realization made her question the morality of their plan and her involvement in it. The discomfort brought on by Zeke's behavior only added to her turmoil.

She knew the importance of staying focused on their objective, yet she couldn't shake off the unease Zeke's actions had caused. The thought of continuing with the plan now felt more daunting than ever.

Maria took a deep breath, trying to find clarity amid the whirlwind of emotions. She needed to reassess her priorities and decide how to navigate the complex situation she found herself in. The night's events had left her at a crossroads, torn between her feelings for me and the plan she had committed to.

Chapter Three

"Bye, Saint Tropez"

The final day in Saint Tropez greeted the group with a radiant sunrise, casting a golden glow over their last moments in the idyllic French town. After a night filled with poolside volleyball, champagne and tequila shots, I found myself relaxed and thankful, as I struggled to get up from bed with Maria beside me.

During breakfast, amidst the farewells, we bade a particularly poignant goodbye to Louisa, who chose to extend her stay in France.

Onboard the private jet bound for San Francisco, the group reflected on their unforgettable experiences. Maria, feeling unwell, gratefully accepted painkillers from me. The flight was filled with nostalgia, laughter, and discussions of future plans.

Cody, already dreaming of their next escapade, proposed another group trip for his upcoming birthday. I was buoyed by the spirit of friendship and new beginnings, and extended a job opportunity to Cody, while Zeke enthusiastically planned our next adventure for Cody's birthday.

Touching down in San Francisco, I received exhilarating news: my dream home in the Oakland Hills was officially mine. The group shared in my excitement, eagerly anticipating the new memories they would create in this vibrant city.

Two weeks later, I had settled into my new home, a stunning architectural marvel in the Oakland Hills. The moment I stepped inside, I was captivated by its elegance and warmth. The grand living area, with its high ceilings and expansive windows, offered a breathtaking view of the San Francisco city skyline. The backyard, with its inviting pool mirroring the city lights, promised countless future gatherings filled with joy and laughter. In this space, I envisioned not just a home, but a sanctuary where new chapters of my life would unfold.

My bedroom was a sanctuary of tranquility, bathed in soothing blues and grays. The majestic window framed an artistic view of the pool and the city beyond, creating a seamless blend of indoor and outdoor serenity. The king-sized bed, decked with plush pillows and crisp white sheets, stood as an inviting promise of restful nights. The en-suite bathroom, featuring a deep soaking tub and a spacious walk-in shower, was a haven for relaxation, beckoning me to unwind in luxury.

As I unpacked, I felt a profound sense of peace enveloping me, a feeling that had been rare in my fast-paced life. I was filled with gratitude for this journey so far and excitement for what the future held. This beautiful home symbolized not just success but the beginning of a new, extraordinary chapter in my life.

Later, in the backyard, a glass of wine in hand, my thoughts rambled to Moji. I imagined how she would have loved this place, the breathtaking view, the inviting pool, every meticulous detail reflecting our shared dreams. I smiled, reminiscing about the times we had spent envisioning our ideal homes, a blend of youthful optimism and aspirations.

My phone chimed, snapping me back to reality. It was Maria. A wave of happiness washed over me as I greeted her.

"Hey Maria, how's everything with you?" I asked, with a warm voice.

Maria's response was equally cheerful. "I'm doing well. Just busy with work. How's the new house?"

"It's more than I could have hoped for. You should come by and see it," I offered, genuinely excited at the idea.

"That sounds great. I actually have some free time today. Mind if I swing by?" Maria inquired.

"Of course! I'll text you the address. See you soon," I replied, my heart lit with anticipation.

The thought of showing Maria my new home thrilled me. It was an opportunity to share a part of my life that was deeply personal and meaningful. As I waited for her arrival, I felt a sense of contentment. The house, with all its elegance and charm, was not just a place of residence; it was a reflection of my dreams and aspirations, now a tangible reality. I looked forward to creating new memories here, and this started with Maria's visit.

As I prepared for Maria's visit, I felt a profound sense of pride and contentment in my new home. The sound of a car pulling up announced her arrival, and I opened the door to greet her. Maria stood there, her expression one of awe and admiration.

"This place is stunning, Femi," she exclaimed, her eyes taking in the elegance and beauty of the surroundings.

"Thanks, Maria. I'm really glad you're here to see it," I replied, my smile genuine, I could feel my face reshape into a smile and back as I welcomed her inside.

We toured the house, our conversation flowing effortlessly. We shared memories of Saint Tropez and updates on our lives wove a tapestry of laughter and warmth. Eventually, we found ourselves outside, captivated by the breathtaking view of the San Francisco skyline.

As the evening sky deepened into twilight, I opened a bottle of wine, and we settled comfortably by the pool. The ambiance was perfect, a blend of comfort, luxury, and the intimacy of our rapidly growing yet slow connection.

Maria, in a playful yet probing tone, teased, "So, have you had other guests over already?"

I chuckled, sensing the underlying question in her jest. "What makes you ask that?"

Maria shrugged, a hint of curiosity in her voice. "I don't know, just wondering."

"Now you don't know?" I teased back, must have had a playful glint in my eye.

I sipped my wine, then turned to Maria with a sincere expression. "Maria, you're the first person I've invited here. No one else, not even the guys, have seen my house yet. I wanted you to be the first because you're special to me. I value our time together, and I've been looking forward to seeing you again. Your presence here means a lot. I don't know what it is but something about you makes being around homely and exciting."

Maria's eyes sparkled, I could tell she was touched by my words. My reassurance was exactly what she needed to hear. In that moment, I gently tilted her chin up and kissed her softly, a gesture that deepened our connection and spoke volumes about our mutual affection.

The evening progressed in a blissful blend of conversation, laughter, and shared moments. We sat by the pool, the city lights twinkling in the distance, it was clear that a new chapter was unfolding in our lives, one filled with potential and promise.

The following morning, Maria rose with the sun, feeling an eagerness to extend her kindness in my new home. Despite the limited options in my pantry, she skillfully prepared a modest but appetizing breakfast of scrambled eggs, waffles, and freshly brewed coffee. Balancing the tray carefully, she made her way to my bedroom, hoping to surprise me with breakfast in bed.

As she entered the room, my eyes lit up with appreciation. "This smells amazing, thank you," I said, sitting up and admiring the thoughtful gesture.

Maria, with a soft smile, leaned in for a gentle kiss. "I wish I could stay longer, but I have family commitments today," she regretfully informed me.

***

After enjoying the breakfast Maria had prepared, I set out for his morning jog. The streets of the Oakland Hills neighborhood offered captivating views of the city and a refreshing start to my day. During my run, I encountered Catherine, a woman whose poise and fitness caught my attention.

"Good morning," she greeted with a friendly smile.

"Morning," I responded, appreciative of the warm interaction.

"I'm Catherine. I've noticed you running here often. Are you new in the neighborhood?" she inquired.

"Yes, I'm Femi. Moved in a couple of weeks ago," I replied, shaking her hand as we both tried to catch our breaths after pausing from the run.

Our conversation flowed naturally, touching on various aspects of the neighborhood and our shared appreciation for the scenic beauty. We exchanged numbers, planning to join each other for future runs, a prospect I found pleasantly inviting.

***

Meanwhile, Maria drove back to her apartment in San Jose, her mind replaying the moments she had shared with me. Our time together had been deeply intimate, leaving her with a longing for more of his presence. As she entered her apartment, a sense of solitude enveloped her, contrasting sharply with the warmth and connection she had felt in my company. Her thoughts lingered on me, wondering about the future and the possibilities it might hold. The mix of emotions was overwhelming, yet she couldn't help but feel a sense of excitement for what lay ahead.

Maria, emerging from her shower and getting dressed, found her thoughts still heavily centered on me. She was aware of the depth of her feelings, which seemed to deepen with every interaction. Despite knowing she should guard her heart, she couldn't help but fantasize about a future with me. She even caught herself imagining living together, though she knew such thoughts were premature.

Trying to ground herself in reality, Maria spent the day with family and took care of household chores. Even as she folded laundry, her mind drifted back to Femi, wondering about the possibilities that a relationship with him could bring.

That evening, I called her to discuss my upcoming housewarming party. I asked for her help in planning the event, an invitation Maria accepted with enthusiasm. It felt like an opportunity to be closer to me, to be part of my life in a new and exciting way.

***

Throughout the week, Catherine and I had established a routine of morning runs. Our conversations were effortless and engaging, I shared aspects of my life and work. Catherine, in turn, opened up about her own life, including her divorce and her love for running. Our bond grew steadily, and I found himself admiring her resilience, strength, and the playful way she challenged me.

I realized I was developing feelings for her, a realization that came with a hint of caution given my past romantic experiences. However, I couldn't deny the connection we shared. With Catherine, it was different, I couldn't place it at first but there was a way she made me feel like a man, like her man and she did it effortlessly.

One morning, after our run, I decided to take a chance. "Catherine, I've really enjoyed our time together. Would you like to go out with me, maybe for dinner?" I asked with a mix of hope and anxiety in my voice.

Catherine's response was a mix of surprise and delight. "I'd love to, Femi. Dinner tonight sounds perfect," she replied, her smile indicating her interest.

We agreed to meet at an Italian bistro, setting the time for our date. "I'll pick you up at 7 pm," I suggested, feeling a sense of excitement building within me.

As I walked away from our departing point, I couldn't help but feel a thrill of anticipation for the evening ahead. I was stepping into new territory, exploring a connection that felt both promising and refreshing. The prospect of getting to know Catherine better, outside the context of our morning runs, was an opportunity I eagerly looked forward to.

I arrived at Catherine's residence that evening which marked the beginning of a memorable night. As she gracefully descended the staircase, her elegance was undeniable. Dressed in a sleek black dress that gave prominence to her poise, Catherine was the epitome of sophistication. I couldn't help but be captivated by her presence.

"You look absolutely stunning," I said, offering her my arm in a gentlemanly gesture as we headed to my car.

Catherine, touched by the compliment, blushed slightly. "Thank you, Femi," she responded, a mix of confidence and modesty in her voice.

Our dinner was filled with engaging conversation and laughter. We connected over shared interests and stories, enjoying a bottle of wine and a delightful array of Italian cuisine. I could tell my culinary choices and ease in navigating the dining experience impressed Catherine, she found herself increasingly drawn to my charisma and confidence.

"Is there anything else on the menu you'd like to try?" I asked, eager to ensure Catherine enjoyed the meal as much as I did.

Catherine was momentarily caught off guard by my attentiveness, and replied, "No, everything's been perfect. You've chosen wonderfully."

As we indulged in the last course, I leaned in closer. "I've really enjoyed our time tonight, Catherine. I'm hoping we can do this again soon."

Catherine's smile was radiant, reflecting her enjoyment of the evening. "I'd love that, Femi. This has been a wonderful night," she said, her eyes sparkling with genuine affection.

Our intimate conversation was momentarily paused as the waiter approached, presenting the dessert menu with a warm smile. "Would you like something sweet to finish your meal?"

Glancing at Catherine, I asked with a playful glint in my eye, "Shall we share a dessert?"

We agreed on a tiramisu, a sweet end to a delightful evening.

As we enjoyed the tiramisu, I lightheartedly suggested a morning run to counteract the indulgence of our dinner. Catherine's laughter and playful agreement filled the air with an ease that I found irresistibly charming.

"I think I might need to speed up a bit to keep up with you tomorrow," she joked, her eyes gleaming with delight.

"Don't worry, I'll adjust my pace. We wouldn't want to overdo it," I replied, my tone teasing yet considerate as my grin broadened.

"Shall we?" I asked after signing the receipt of their dinner.

The drive back to Catherine's home was filled with a comfortable silence, punctuated by brief exchanges and shared smiles. I felt a connection that was both exciting and new, and wasn't ready for the evening to end. As we reached her door, I expressed my hope for another evening like this.

Catherine, unlocking her door, turned to me with a sincere smile. "I had a wonderful time tonight, Femi. Thank you."

Acting on impulse, I leaned in and gently kissed her cheek. "Sleep well," I murmured, stepping back.

Catherine's response was a playful suggestion, her eyes inviting. "Why don't you come in for a glass of wine?"

Tempted, with no hesitation I followed her inside, the door closing behind us. Inside, the mood shifted from playful to intimate. Catherine opened a bottle of wine, poured me a glass before excusing herself to change, leaving me momentarily alone.

When she returned, I was taken aback by her elegance and allure. She had changed into something more comfortable, yet undeniably captivating. Her appearance took my breath away. I don't know how this forty-five old woman has me in her hands so fast, I'm helpless. "Get it together Femi," I said to myself as I snapped back to life.

"You look stunning," I managed to say, my voice barely above a whisper.

Catherine blushed at my compliment, "thank God she heard me," as I continued to talk to myself. Her confidence mingled with a hint of vulnerability. "Thank you," she said softly.

Our embrace was natural and full of an unspoken understanding. She held my hand and led me back to where I was seated, like an obedient dog, I followed her, my tail wagging in joy. She picked up the bottle of wine, refilled my glass, handled it over to me and seconds later sat on my lap. Whispered sweet words in my ear as she played with short curls and kissed my neck. Her hand slowly and gently rubbing on arm encouraged to keep drinking. I didn't know when I downed the wine in my glass, I was a gunner with no control and she could tell. Her lips soon made their way to mine, as we kissed, there was a sense of deepening connection, a feeling that this night was the start of something meaningful.

In the early hours of the morning, I quietly dressed, careful not to disturb Catherine. I felt a mix of emotions as I prepared to leave, contentment from the night's experiences but also a tinge of regret for not staying longer.

As I opened the door to leave the room, I paused, looked back one last time. Catherine laid there, peaceful and unaware, a serene contrast to the whirlwind of emotions I felt. I made my way to the front door, each step echoing with the memories of the night. Stepping out into the dawn, I closed the door behind me, carrying with me the memories of a night that had unexpectedly touched my heart and my shoes.

As I walked to my car, parked a short distance away, I found myself lost in thought. The evening had been an unexpected whirlwind of emotions, a dance of connection and vulnerability with Catherine that left me elated yet introspective. The guilt of departing without a proper goodbye tugged at me, mixing with the thrill of a newfound intimacy.

As I navigated the quiet streets, I acknowledged the need for contemplation. Our relationship, however promising, was still fragile, a delicate balance that required careful consideration. The excitement of the evening lingered, but so did a sense of responsibility towards what might become.

For now, I chose to immerse myself in the afterglow of the night, savoring the memories while mentally preparing for the workday ahead. The drive back home was contemplative, a journey not just through the streets of Oakland Hills but through my own thoughts and feelings. The night had been a leap into uncharted territory, and as I parked my car and stepped out, I knew that the coming days would be crucial in determining the path of my relationship with Catherine.

***

I arrived at my company's headquarters in downtown San Francisco, still feeling the aftereffects of my late-night encounter with Catherine. Settling into my office, I sipped coffee and began my workday, though my thoughts periodically drifted back to the previous evening.

As the day progressed, I regained my usual focus and energy, efficiently tackling my tasks. Yet, my mind often wandered to Catherine, pondering if she was going to join me on our runs after our newly uncharted territory.

"Hey bro, you got time to grab lunch with me?" I asked, my excitement must have lit Zeke's office cause I felt the energy reciprocated.

"I sure can. Welcome back!" Zeke closed his laptop and joined me. We embraced after our handshake and headed to lunch.

During lunch, I caught Zeke up with what had been going on with me at a nearby café. Despite our different upbringing and cultural difference, we shared a bond over our mutual interests in life, technology and entrepreneurship which all started from pickup basketball games for students who didn't make the college basketball team but we found a new brotherhood and friendship in one another.

Zeke greeted me with a friendly smile. "How's it going, man?"

"Pretty well," I replied. "I've been settling into Oakland Hills nicely. Met someone interesting too."

Zeke's curiosity piqued. "Oh? Do tell."

I shared details about Catherine, our dinner date, how I snuck out in the early hours of the morning and the connection we had formed. Zeke listened, amused and intrigued by my newfound romantic interest.

"Planning to see her again?" Zeke inquired.

"Definitely," I confirmed. "I'm thinking of inviting her to my housewarming party. What do you think?"

Zeke nodded in approval. "Sounds like a good plan."

I chuckled, pleased with my recent adventures. However, Zeke's next question gave me a pause.

"Isn't Maria going to be there too?" he asked.

Realizing the potential complication, I acknowledged Maria's significant role in organizing the event. "I'll need to figure something out," I mused.

The rest of lunch was silent after Zeke's question.

Back at the office, I reached out to both Maria and Catherine via text, navigating the delicate balance between my growing connection with Catherine and my existing relationship with Maria.

Maria's response indicated she had everything under control for the party, while Catherine's message expressed her enjoyment of our time together and anticipation for our next run.

Zeke, dropping by my office, teased me about Maria. I played it cool, focusing on the remainder of his work.

As the day wound down, I found myself at a crossroads. My new relationship with Catherine was exciting but complicated, and my connection with Maria, though initially part of a plan, had grown into something more meaningful. I realized that navigating these relationships would require careful thought and consideration to ensure I didn't hurt anyone involved, including myself. The upcoming housewarming party, with both women in attendance, would undoubtedly be a pivotal moment in determining the course of these complex relationships.

Chapter Four

"Housewarming Party - The House of the Demon"

The morning of my housewarming party I found myself buzzing with excitement and a touch of nerves. I was up early, busying myself in the kitchen with preparations for the appetizers. My phone buzzed with a message from Maria.

"Good morning, Femi! Do you need any help before the party starts?"

Maria had been instrumental in planning the event, taking care of the catering and drink arrangements. I quickly replied, expressing my gratitude and assuring her that everything was under control.

Shortly after, the catering team arrived, promptly getting to work setting up for the event. I was impressed by their professionalism and efficiency, which allowed me to focus on other aspects of the party preparation.

In the midst of my preparations, I received a text from a friend, eagerly asking about the party's start time. It was a reminder that the celebration was drawing near, and I needed to get ready.

As I finished dressing, another message from Maria popped up, confirming the arrival and setup of the drinks in the backyard. I smiled, appreciative of her diligent efforts.

Descending to inspect the party setup, I was pleased to see everything coming together perfectly. The backyard was transformed into a festive space with string lights, colorful balloons, and a well-stocked drinks table featuring an array of choices.

Feeling a sense of accomplishment, I allowed myself a moment to take it all in. This was my first housewarming party in my new home, a milestone I was eager to share with my friends. I took a deep breath, reminding myself to relax and enjoy the festivities.

Maria arrived early to lend a final hand. She had dedicated the past week to ensuring every detail was perfect for my party. After assisting the catering team with the setup, she meticulously arranged the bar area, eager for the guests to enjoy the evening.

As the party's start time approached, guests began to arrive. Cody was among the first, looking sharp in his suit. Maria greeted him with her usual warmth, directing him to the bar for a drink.

The housewarming party at my new Oakland Hills home was in full swing, with guests mingling and music filling the air. Maria, who had been instrumental in planning the event, received compliments from Cody on her exceptional efforts. She humbly attributed her hard work to making the party perfect for me.

As more guests arrived, including Zeke, Chidi, and Khadi, the atmosphere grew even livelier. They were all impressed by my beautiful home and the stunning view of the city. I was basking in the success of the party and the warmth of my friends, I expressed my gratitude for their presence.

***

Catherine's arrival added a new dimension to the evening. Dressed in a striking red dress, her appearance captivated everyone, especially me. Maria greeted her warmly, but couldn't help feeling a twinge of jealousy at the undeniable chemistry between her and me.

I was momentarily lost in Catherine's allure, I quickly regained my composure and complimented her on her stunning look. Our easy banter and laughter indicated a deepening connection, which didn't go unnoticed by Maria.

As the evening progressed, I introduced Catherine to my friends. The group engaged in lively conversations, and it was clear that Catherine was fitting in seamlessly.

Maria, observing Catherine and I, felt a mix of emotions. She tried to focus on enjoying the party, but the sight of Catherine and I together stirred feelings she struggled to suppress.

***

Later, Catherine and I found ourselves on the patio, alone under the starlit sky. The city lights below us added a magical backdrop to our intimate conversation.

"I'm really glad you're here, Catherine," I said, my voice reflecting my genuine feelings.

Catherine's eyes reflecting the city lights, responded with equal sincerity. "This is an amazing place, Femi. I'm happy to be here with you."

Our moment on the patio was one of connection and potential, a hint of something deeper developing between us as she slightly lay her head on my shoulder. My hand was on her waist, it felt like it was used to being there. Our silence had more volume than the music playing inside the house.

"Don't think I forgave you for sneaking out without letting me know," Catherine broke the silence and love tapped my chest.

We both laughed as we headed back inside, where Khadi and Chidi danced with a passion that was both infectious and inspiring. Their relationship, blossoming beautifully, was a testament to the power of love made in Saint Tropez.

I seized the opportunity to show Catherine around my home, and led her on a tour. Each room we entered, Catherine expressed her admiration for my taste and the effort I had put into making the house a home.

"This house reflects you, Femi. It's beautiful, thoughtful, and welcoming," Catherine commented, her eyes scanning the carefully curated spaces.

"Thank you," I replied, a sense of pride in my voice. "I wanted it to be a place where friends could gather and make memories."

As we continued our tour, the connection between us deepened. We shared stories and insights, each room sparking new topics of conversation. The night was evolving into an intimate exploration of my world, with Catherine showing genuine interest and appreciation.

Back on the dance floor, the energy was high, and the guests were thoroughly enjoying themselves. Maria, though distracted by her own complex emotions, managed to mingle and ensure that everyone was having a good time.

My housewarming party was shaping up to be a night of celebration, connections, and perhaps the beginning of new relationships. As we continued our tour, the potential for something special between us grew, leaving me with a sense of anticipation for what the future might hold.

Catherine's appreciation for my taste in décor was evident. The luxurious furniture, high ceilings, and carefully selected artwork throughout the house reflected my attention to detail and style.

"Your house is absolutely stunning, Femi. You have great taste," Catherine complimented, her eyes shining with admiration.

"Thank you," I responded, pleased by her reaction. "I'm glad you like it."

Our stroll through the house brought us to the main bedroom, where Catherine was taken aback by the impressive view of the city. "This is just breathtaking," she said, turning to me with a smile.

I acknowledge her comment with a smile. "It's not just the house that matters, but the people you share it with," I said, emphasizing the importance of companionship over material possessions.

"I've always wanted to ask you what the tattoo on your left arm meant," she said, her fingers slowly making their way to my hand.

"This?" I pointed to the tattoo I believed she was referring to.

"Yeah, Femi. What does the ECC 9:6-9 mean?" Her body pressing on mine.

"It's the code I live my life by," I responded.

"What is this code, mysterious man?" She was now really curious.

"It's a quote in the bible from the book of Ecclesiastes. I will read you the last verse," I said with a smirk on my face. "Enjoy life with the woman you love, as long as you live the life that God has given you in this world. Enjoy every day of it, because that is all you will get for all your trouble." I paused, pulled her towards me and told her, "you are the woman I love, I know you are worth the trouble of life."

"I learn something new about you every time," she looked at me with so much admiration in her eyes.

Our eyes were locked on each other, you would have needed something sharper than a knife to cut the tension in the room.

Our exchange in the main bedroom was a moment that led to a quick passion, a sense of belonging, mutual understanding as we shared a kiss, hot for each other and attraction growing between us. I knew she had no underwear on when she laid her head on my chest at the patio so I knew what to do when this moment came. Surprisingly so did she, my belt unbuckled by her, my trousers fell down my laps, I turned her around, her dress raised above her waist and she guided me into her before falling to the bed for support as I thrusted her.

"I hope your housewarming gift was warm enough?" She asked as she pulled her dress down coming from the bathroom.

I had this huge smile on my face, "Yes, it was. Warm and juicy," I said as I continued to catch my breath.

Meanwhile, back in the living room, the atmosphere was lively, with music and laughter filling the air. Khadi and Chidi were the center of attention, dancing closely, lost in their own world. Khadi rested her head against Chidi's chest, reveling in the comfort and security of his embrace.

"I could get used to this," Khadi said softly, looking up at Chidi with affection.

Chidi's response was tender, his love for Khadi evident in his smile and the gentle kiss he planted on her forehead. The couple's affection for each other was a beautiful sight, a testament to the deep bond they had formed.

In the kitchen, Maria was busy ensuring the drinks were perfectly arranged for the guests. Realizing that I was not in the immediate vicinity, she decided to find me, wondering if I needed any assistance. She approached Chidi and Khadi, and inquired about my whereabouts.

"He's probably giving a tour of the house," Chidi responded, his arms affectionately wrapped around Khadi.

Acknowledging Chidi's response, Maria made her way toward the stairs. As she approached, she felt a gentle pull on her hand and turned to see Zeke. He appeared to have something important to discuss and gestured for a more private conversation.

"Can we talk for a minute?" Zeke asked in a serious tone, glancing around to ensure privacy.

Surprised, Maria agreed, curious about the nature of his concern. "Sure, what's up?"

"It's about you and Femi," Zeke began, his voice low. "I've noticed you two have been spending a lot of time together. I'm just curious to know where you are with our plan."

Maria furrowed her brow. "What do you mean?"

"I mean, when are you planning to get pregnant, remember you need to get pregnant for him?" Zeke asked bluntly.

Maria's eyes widened. "Excuse me?"

"You heard me," Zeke said. "I know you like him but I don't give a fuck. Get pregnant for him fast before Catherine does."

Maria's eyes still widened. "That old lady! Is he fucking her?"

Maria felt her stomach knot as she considered the weight of Zeke's words. She didn't want to feel rushed or pressured into having a baby before she was ready. "I understand that, Zeke, but I don't want to rush things. Having a baby is a significant decision, and I want to make sure I'm prepared for it."

"I get that, but if Femi ends up with Catherine," Zeke said, his voice barely above a whisper, "you know how he is with women. I'm not sure what he sees in Catherine but I know she has caught his attention. If she gets pregnant before you do, you are not going to like me Maria"

A pang of jealousy hit Maria at the mention of Catherine's name, but she tried not to let it show. "I thought she was just friends with Femi."

"I know, but I've seen the way he looks at her," Zeke said, his expression grave. "I don't want you to lose out to her. I don't want to take drastic measures, but if I lose to Catherine or any other woman before I can execute my plans, I won't need you around. I'll make sure you're out of the picture for a long time." Zeke's words hung heavily in the air as he walked away, hands in his pockets, forcing a fake smile as he disappeared from Maria's view.

Maria felt a wave of anger wash over her. She couldn't believe that Zeke was putting so much pressure on her to get pregnant. She took a deep breath, trying to calm herself down. After a couple of minutes, she managed a smile, feeling a little better now that the tension had dissipated, and rejoined the party.

***

As Catherine and I descended the stairs, our faces were alight with the joy of having shared a special moment together. The party had dwindled down to a few guests, creating a more intimate atmosphere in the living room.

Khadi and Chidi, still engrossed in their dance, seemed to be in a world of their own, a testament to their deepening relationship. I scanned the room, noticing that Zeke and Maria were not in sight, and wondered if they had left the party during my absence.

Maria, from her spot near the drinks table, felt a surge of discomfort as she saw Catherine and I rejoining the party. Despite her efforts to manage her feelings of jealousy, after seeing us together, so evidently happy and close, stirred up emotions she had been trying to keep at bay.

Catherine was on a high, having spent an intimate and meaningful time with me. Her feelings for me had deepened, and the moment we had shared was

something she cherished. However, she couldn't help
but notice Maria's distant demeanor.

Seeking to ease any tension, Catherine approached
Maria. "Is everything okay?" she inquired with
genuine concern.

Maria, masking her true feelings, offered a strained
smile. "Yeah, I'm just a bit tired," she replied, hoping
to maintain a semblance of normalcy.

Catherine, sensing something amiss but not wanting
to pry, suggested perhaps it was time to wind the
party down. However, she couldn't help but turn to
me with a playful question about our plans for the
rest of the evening.

I was caught up in the spirit of the party, and
responded with humor. "Let's just enjoy the moment.
We've stirred up enough excitement for one night."

Catherine's playful pout was met with my amused
refusal. "Don't make it too obvious, you just had a
chocolate bar with a vanilla topping woman, keep it
together," I thought to myself. Her flirtatious remark
about being ready for more adventures elicited a laugh
from me. "You really are insatiable," I teased.

Catherine's response, a mix of flirtation and humor, highlighted the chemistry between me. "Guilty as charged," she said, her grin infectious.

The party continued in a lighter mood, the tension momentarily forgotten. Laughter and conversation filled the room, as the remaining guests savored the final moments of the night.

Throughout the evening, Maria maintained her composure as the gracious hostess, seamlessly blending into her role. She circulated among the guests, offering drinks and engaging in light conversation, all while keeping a watchful eye on Catherine and I. Despite her internal conflict, she managed to hide her true feelings, projecting an aura of calm and hospitality.

The complexity of her emotions, however, was a silent storm brewing within her. She couldn't help but feel a pang of jealousy every time she saw Catherine and I together, our easy camaraderie and laughter a stark reminder of her own uncertain standing with Femi. Yet, she was determined not to let these feelings overshadow the evening.

The arrival of Taylor, Cody's date, introduced a new dynamic to the gathering. Maria observed their interaction, noticing the natural chemistry between them. It was a bittersweet moment for her, seeing another potential love story unfold while grappling with her own feelings of uncertainty about me.

As the night progressed, the atmosphere of the party remained lively and upbeat. Guests mingled, shared stories, and enjoyed the music, creating a joyous backdrop to the evening. I seemed to be thoroughly enjoying myself, often I was laughing and chatting with Catherine and other guests.

Maria did her best to focus on the success of the party, taking pride in the smooth flow of the evening. However, her thoughts continually drifted back to me and the nature of our relationship. The night had started as a celebration of my new home, but for Maria, it had evolved into a night of introspection and realization about her feelings for me.

Khadi noticed that Maria was not her usual happy self. Excusing herself from Chidi, Khadi made her way over to Maria and gently placed a hand on her shoulder.

"Hey, is everything okay?" Khadi asked, concern etched on her face.

Maria shook her head and whispered, "No, not really. Zeke is blackmailing me, and I don't know what to do. And now with Catherine here, I feel like she's a threat to my relationship with Femi."

"What? Zeke is blackmailing you? Why?" Khadi asked incredulously.

Maria felt a lump form in her throat as she tried to explain the situation. "I don't know how to explain it to you. And now with Catherine here, I feel like Femi's attention is divided."

Khadi listened intently, feeling a mix of anger and sympathy towards Maria. She couldn't believe that Zeke would stoop so low as to blackmail someone to get what he wanted.

"That's a tough situation. But you can't let Zeke manipulate you like that. And as for Catherine, Femi is a grown man; he can make his own decisions. You just have to trust in your relationship with him," Khadi said, placing a comforting arm around Maria's shoulders.

Maria nodded, feeling grateful for Khadi's support. "Thanks, Khadi. I know you're right. I just needed to talk to someone about it."

"Of course, anytime. We're all here for you," Khadi replied with a reassuring smile.

As they made their way back to the party, Maria felt a weight lifted off her shoulders. She knew the situation with Zeke and Catherine was far from over, and she hadn't shared the whole truth with Khadi. But for now, she was going to enjoy the party and the time she had with Femi.

Maria and Khadi's friendship was one of those rare bonds that seemed to withstand the test of time and circumstance. Their journey began in the vibrant neighborhoods of San Jose, California, where they grew up just a few blocks apart in homes to immigrant parents. Their paths first crossed in elementary school, where they quickly became inseparable, sharing a deep affinity for creativity and a zest for life that made them stand out.

Throughout their school years, Maria and Khadi were known for their unwavering support for each other. Whether it was school projects, sports events, or navigating the trials of adolescence, they were always there for one another. They shared countless memories, from sleepovers filled with laughter and dreams to days spent exploring the bustling streets of San Jose.

Their bond deepened as they entered high school, a period marked by significant growth and change. Despite their evolving interests – Khadi gravitating towards literature and the arts, while Maria showed a keen interest in science and technology, their friendship remained strong. They were a familiar sight in the school corridors, known for their lively discussions and infectious energy.

Even when it was time to choose colleges, fate seemed to align in their favor. Both Maria and Khadi ended up attending colleges in California, not too far from each other. This proximity allowed them to maintain their close connection, meeting up often, sharing their college experiences, and supporting each other through academic and personal challenges.

Their friendship was more than just shared history; it was a deep understanding and acceptance of each other. Maria always admired Khadi's intelligence and determination, while Khadi respected Maria's creativity and empathetic nature. Together, they balanced each other out, offering perspectives and support that enriched their lives.

As they transitioned into adulthood, their friendship evolved but never wavered. They continued to share their hopes, dreams, and even uncertainties about the future. This enduring friendship was a testament to their mutual respect, understanding, and the shared experiences that had shaped them from their early days in San Jose to the present.

Now, as they found themselves at my housewarming party, it was yet another chapter in their long-standing friendship. Maria, despite her current internal conflicts, knew she had a steadfast ally in Khadi, someone who had been with her through thick and thin, a friend who was more like family.

After her conversation with Khadi, Maria still felt a lingering sense of unease. Despite her attempts to shake off her concerns about Zeke and Catherine, her mind was clouded with doubts. Pushing these thoughts to the back of her mind, she decided to immerse herself in the festivities of the party. As she made her way back to the heart of the gathering, she noticed I was engaged in conversation with an unfamiliar guest. Seizing the opportunity, Maria approached me.

"Hey, stranger," she greeted me with a warm, undeniably slightly forced, smile.

I turned to her, my face lighting up with genuine pleasure. "Hey, Maria. I was just talking about you. Thanks for everything you've done today."

Maria brushed off the compliment with a casual, "Of course, anything for you. Are you enjoying yourself?"

"Yeah, it's been fantastic," I responded, glancing around at the successful party. "I'm just glad it's all going smoothly."

Nodding in agreement, Maria decided to seize the moment. "Would you like to dance?"

My response was immediate and enthusiastic. "I'd love to."

Together, we moved to the dance floor, where the lively beat of an afrobeats song welcomed us. As we began to dance, the rest of the guests formed a circle around us, cheering and clapping. Both Maria and I are skilled dancers, our movements in sync with the rhythm, our chemistry evident to all onlookers.

For Maria, the dance was a much-needed diversion. The rhythm and my presence momentarily eased her anxieties, allowing her to enjoy the present. As we swayed and moved together, she felt a sense of ownership over me on the dancefloor, her dance moves were more of a statement.

The song eventually came to an end, and with a genuine smile, I thanked Maria. "That was incredible," I said, my voice filled with appreciation. "I really needed that."

Maria, her spirits lifted by the dance, replied, "Me too. I'm glad we could share that moment."

Just as they were about to part ways, Catherine approached them, a polite yet somewhat uneasy smile on her face. "Hey, guys," she said. "I've been looking for you."

As the ever gracious host, I responded with a smile. "We were just enjoying the dance floor. Did you want to join us?"

Catherine hesitated, her eyes briefly flicking to Maria. "Actually, I wanted to talk to you, Femi. Just for a second. Alone, if that's okay."

Maria felt a familiar twinge of jealousy but masked it with a courteous smile. "No problem, go ahead," she said, stepping back to give them space.

As I excused myself to speak with Catherine, Maria was left with a mix of emotions. The joy of the dance was quickly overshadowed by the uncertainty of what Catherine's private conversation with Femi might entail.

As I walked Catherine to the door, our conversation winding down, she was ready to call it a night. We exchanged a few last words. I expressed my hopes that she would enjoy her upcoming trip to New York and get the chance to see her daughter, CeCe. However, just as we were about to say our goodbyes, a knock on the door interrupted us.

I opened the door and found two police officers standing outside. The sound of the party had apparently been too loud for one of the neighbors, who had lodged a noise complaint.

"Excuse me, sir," one of the officers said to me. "We've received a complaint about loud noise coming from this address. Can we come in and have a look around?"

I glanced at Catherine, a look of mild embarrassment crossing my face. "Sure, officers. Please come in," I said, stepping aside to allow them entry.

Catherine, understanding the gravity of the situation, reassured me with a smile. "It's alright. I've had a great time anyway," she said, offering support.

Inside, the party atmosphere had shifted noticeably. The guests' expressions ranged from unease to curiosity as the officers began their inspection. Maria, watching from a distance, felt a knot form in her stomach. She was concerned about the potential impact of this incident on my reputation and our relationship.

The officers, both tall and imposing figures, introduced themselves and explained their presence. While one maintained a stern demeanor, the other seemed more relaxed but still professional. They moved through the house, ensuring there were no signs of illegal activity or serious disturbances.

I was still in host mode, attempting to diffuse the situation with my charm, explaining the nature of the gathering. However, the officers remained focused on their duty, not swayed by my attempts at lightening the mood.

After a few tense minutes, the officers concluded that the noise level had subsided and that the party posed no further disturbance. They advised me to keep the volume down in the future before preparing to leave.

"Thank you for your cooperation," one of the officers said as they headed towards the door. "Just keep the noise to a minimum, please."

"Absolutely, officer. Thank you," I responded, visibly relieved that the situation had been resolved without further complications.

The mood in the house had undeniably changed following the police visit. Guests began to murmur among themselves, the earlier excitement giving way to a more subdued atmosphere.

I apologized to Catherine for the unexpected interruption. "I'm sorry about this. Not exactly how I wanted the night to end," I said, a hint of frustration in my voice.

Catherine gave me a reassuring smile. "Don't worry about it. These things happen. I still had a great time."

As we said our final goodbyes, I accompanied Catherine to her car, ensuring she left safely. Returning to the house, I found Maria and the remaining guests in a reflective mood.

The unexpected visit from the police had put a damper on the evening, but it had also brought the group closer together in a shared experience. As the last of the guests prepared to leave, Maria and I found ourselves alone, the echoes of the night's events lingering in the air.

In the quiet aftermath, I turned to Maria. "Are you okay?" I asked, noticing the concern in her eyes.

Maria, her emotions a mix of relief and reflection, nodded. "Yeah, it's just been an eventful night."

I wrapped an arm around her, offering comfort. "I'm glad we got to dance, at least. That was a highlight for me."

Maria smiled, leaning into me. "It was nice, wasn't it? Thanks for that."

Maria closed her eyes, savoring every sensation of my tender kisses.

I picked her up, intending to carry her up the stairs, but then shook my head and set her back down.

"What, you're not going to carry me up to the room?" Maria asked, feeling a little confused.

"I need the energy for what we are about to do in the room," I responded playfully.

"You'll have to catch me then," Maria teased as she dashed up the stairs to the bedroom.

I chased after her, both laughing and breathless. She was in nothing but her bra and panties as I got to the room. She walked slowly like a lioness looking to trap her prey, catwalking, tiptoeing to the otherside of the room. I watched as she swung her ass cheeks in both directions effortlessly, like they were lost and needed direction and I was in charge of giving them directions, the director. That night, we lost ourselves in each other's embrace, our love and passion deepening with every touch.

Chapter Five

"O Ye Ezekiel - Their hearts are greedy for unjust gain"

Maria awoke to the comforting warmth of the sun streaming through the blinds of my bedroom. Turning to her side, she saw me sleeping peacefully, a serene expression on my face. The memories of our passionate night together brought a smile to her lips, filling her heart with a blend of affection and contentment.

As she got up and started getting dressed, a glint of silver caught her eye. It was a delicate bracelet with small charms, lying on the dresser. Maria recognized it instantly — it was similar to the one Catherine had worn at the party. A wave of jealousy surged through her, but she pushed it aside, choosing not to disturb the peace of the morning with her concerns.

Instead, Maria decided to express her feelings in a different way. She went downstairs and prepared a hearty breakfast of eggs, bacon, and toast, her way of showing me how much she cared for me.

I woke up to the aroma of breakfast, came downstairs and greeted Maria with a tender embrace and a soft kiss on her neck. My voice was low and husky, "Good morning."

Maria smiled warmly at me, "Good morning. I made breakfast for us."

My appreciation was evident as I surveyed the breakfast spread. "This looks amazing. Thank you," I said, sitting at the table.

We enjoyed our breakfast together in a comfortable silence, simply appreciating each other's presence. As we finished, my expression turned serious. I took Maria's hand and looked into her eyes.

"Maria, I want you to know how much you mean to me," I began, my voice earnest. "I care about you so much, and your help with the party meant the world to me."

Maria's heart swelled with emotion. She whispered, "I care about you too."

Our kiss was gentle yet filled with emotion, a confirmation of our deepening feelings. As they parted, my eyes sparkled with happiness. "I have a surprise for you," I announced, rising from the table.

I returned with a small velvet box, placed in front of Maria. "Open it," I encouraged, with my grin widening.

Maria's hands trembled slightly as she opened the box. Inside lay a stunning gold necklace with a heart-shaped pendant. Overwhelmed, she murmured, "It's beautiful."

I placed the necklace around her neck, my fingers brushing her skin. "It's a token of my appreciation and affection for you," I said softly.

Tears welled up in Maria's eyes as she gazed at me. She touched the pendant, feeling the weight of my gesture. She knew then that her feelings for me had deepened into something profound.

After breakfast, Maria gathered her belongings to leave. I walked her to the door, where we shared a lingering, affectionate kiss goodbye.

As Maria drove away, her mind was a whirlwind of emotions. She couldn't help but feel conflicted about the bracelet she had seen. Why was it in Femi's bedroom? She touched the pendant of her new necklace, trying to hold onto the beautiful moment they had shared, not wanting to taint it with doubts and suspicions.

The morning had been a mix of love and uncertainty, leaving Maria to ponder the complexities of her relationship with me. She drove off, her thoughts oscillating between the joy of their connection and the unsettling questions that lingered in her mind.

***

Maria's drive home was interrupted by persistent calls from Zeke. Initially, she tried to ignore them, focusing on navigating through the heavy traffic. However, when a text from Zeke popped up on her dashboard, insisting she pick up, she knew she couldn't avoid the conversation any longer.

"Hello! Hey, sorry, I was just trying to focus on the road," Maria said as she finally answered his call.

Zeke's voice carried a tone of irritation. "Yeah! Whatever you say," he replied, dismissively brushing off her excuse.

"So what's up?" Maria inquired, trying to sound casual despite the tension she sensed in his voice.

"I need to talk to you, and it has to be in person. You still know where I live, right?" Zeke's words carried an urgency that Maria couldn't ignore.

"Yeah, I know where you live. I can swing by later this evening, around 5:30 PM?" she suggested, hoping that would suffice.

However, Zeke was insistent. "No, it can't wait. I need to see you now."

A brief silence followed, amplifying the tension between them. Zeke's impatience grew, his voice rising. "Hello! Hello? Did you hear me?"

Maria, feigning a poor connection, responded, "I can hear you now. What did you say?"

Zeke was not in the mood for delays. "I said it can't wait. I need to see you right away."

"It will take me almost an hour to get to Inner Richmond," Maria stated, trying to buy herself some time.

Zeke ended the call abruptly, his frustration evident. "I guess I'll see you in an hour then."

After hanging up, Zeke muttered to himself, "This girl thinks I'm joking. She better not try me. This is serious."

Maria, still on the road, felt a sense of unease. The urgency in Zeke's voice was unsettling, and she couldn't help but wonder what was so important that it couldn't wait. His demanding tone was unusual, and it left her with a feeling of apprehension about what the meeting could entail.

As she continued her drive, her thoughts were a mix of curiosity and concern. The morning had started with a warm feeling of closeness with me, but now she found herself being pulled into what seemed like a potentially stressful situation with Zeke.

What could Zeke possibly want to discuss so urgently? Maria's drive towards Inner Richmond was filled with apprehension. Her thoughts whirled with possibilities about Zeke's urgent summons. What could he possibly need to discuss that was so pressing? As she navigated the busy streets, her anxiety grew with each mile. The day, which had started with the warmth of Femi's company, was taking an unforeseen and unsettling turn.

Upon arriving at Zeke's apartment, the feeling of unease deepened. Zeke and Maria had a long history, and she knew all too well that his intentions were often masked by ulterior motives. As she stepped into his living room, she found him waiting, an air of agitation about him.

"Maria, you're late," Zeke greeted her sternly. "I've been waiting for almost an hour."

"I'm sorry, Zeke," Maria replied, trying to maintain her composure despite the accusatory tone of his voice. "I had to take care of something before coming here."

"Well, you should have called," Zeke retorted, his voice growing even more stern. "I don't like waiting."

Maria could sense the tension in the room, feeling increasingly anxious about what Zeke was up to. She decided to confront the situation head-on. "What do you want, Zeke?" she asked, her voice cautious yet firm.

Zeke's response was direct and shocking. "I want you to listen to the full plan of how we are going to take over Femi's company."

Maria was taken aback by his blunt statement. "Is that why you disrupted my day?" she asked, confusion and disbelief in her voice.

Zeke began to explain his plan, revealing his manipulative intentions behind her meeting with me. "I set you guys up because I knew Femi was your type, and I was sure he'd fall for you, and not to forget our little secret," Zeke admitted. "And now, he's texted me, talking about how much he likes you. My plan is working, but I need you fully on board."

Maria listened, stunned. Zeke's revelation was a betrayal of her trust, a manipulation of her feelings for Femi. He continued, expressing his concerns about Catherine being a potential threat to his plans.

As Zeke refilled his drink, Maria struggled to find the words to respond. She was speechless, her mind racing to process the enormity of Zeke's scheme.

Returning to his seat, Zeke delved deeper into his plot. "I need to take over FemCo Enterprise for my revenge. Femi, unknowingly, played a part in a tragedy that took my sister away."

Maria's heart sank. "But Femi and Keisha never even met each other," she protested, unable to fathom the connection.

Zeke's response was filled with bitterness. "That's where you're wrong. The truth is far more complex."

Maria sat there, her drink untouched, as Zeke began to unravel a story that threatened to shatter everything she believed about me. The revelations that followed were a mix of past pain, hidden secrets, and a quest for vengeance that had ensnared them all.

The day, which had started with a sense of new beginnings with Femi, was now veering into a dark past that Maria had never known. She braced herself as Zeke unfolded a tale of loss, betrayal, and a deep-seated need for revenge that was set to change the course of their lives.

Zeke's story unfolded, his voice heavy with the weight of memories. "Two years ago, Keisha was studying at UC Davis. She often visited me, usually every other weekend. I never introduced her to Femi. I knew his reputation, how girls flocked around him, and I wanted to keep Keisha away from that environment."

Maria listened intently, her confusion growing. She couldn't yet see where Zeke's narrative was leading.

"On my birthday, Keisha came to surprise me. She wasn't supposed to come, but she showed up with a cake. I remember the moment she knocked and opened the door to my dorm room. I was so focused on keeping her out, but she entered with a friend of hers. Later, we all decided to go out to a club, and Keisha and her friend came along."

Zeke paused, taking a sip of his drink as he seemed to gather his thoughts. Maria waited, her heart pounding with anticipation.

"I got so drunk that night, I barely remembered anything. The next morning, I realized Keisha hadn't slept in my room as she usually did when she visited. I called her several times, but there was no answer. While nursing a hangover, I went downstairs to grab some coffee."

He pointed to his head, indicating the intensity of his hangover. Maria could sense the change in Zeke's tone, a mixture of pain and bitterness creeping into his voice.

"I was on my way back to my room, coffee in hand, when I saw Keisha and her friend stepping out of Femi's room. I was paralyzed, unable to process what I was seeing. They didn't see me, so I stayed silent, just watching in shock."

Maria's eyes widened. She could feel the tension in Zeke's words, the sense of betrayal he must have felt.

"After they were out of sight, I went to Femi's room. I knocked, and I heard Femi ask if 'they' were back. His disappointment was evident when he saw it was just me. I remember asking him, 'Who were you expecting?'"

"The two girls that were with us from last night, they spent the night with the Femz," Femi licked his lips rubbing his hands together.

I knew within me that what I was going to hear wasn't what I'd like but I inquired further, "they spend the night doing what?"

"Bro, why are you acting like you don't what happens when two girls spend the night with Femz? We had a threesome, the petite one didn't want to join, I think she was shy or something but after she heard how I was taking care of her friend who was the wild one, she joined. She was a little freak, she just needed time to open up and as soon as she hopped on me, she didn't give her friend any more time to get on top. These girls don't like sharing this steak and I don't blame 'em," Femi concluded.

I didn't know when tears filled my eyes as he described his sexual activities with Keisha. "That is my sister," I said but my lips didn't move. I must have said that out loud in my head but I was the only one who could hear me. I excused myself from his room, I went to a corner in the dorm and cried before gathering myself and went back to my room.

Zeke took another sip of his drink, his gaze distant as he recounted the painful memory. "That moment changed everything. I never confronted Keisha about it. I couldn't bring myself to. But it ate away at me, the thought of her with Femi."

Maria sat there, her drink forgotten, as she tried to piece together the implications of Zeke's story. The revelation that Keisha had been involved with Femi, even if just for a night, was shocking. She could see the pain in Zeke's eyes, the unresolved feelings that were driving his need for revenge.

"And now," Zeke continued, his voice hardening, "I need to make Femi pay for what he did. For how he disrespected my sister, for the pain he indirectly caused. That's why I need you, Maria. That's why this plan is so important to me."

Maria was speechless, her mind racing. The story Zeke had just revealed added a complex layer to her relationship with me. She was torn between the man she was falling for and the vengeful plans of a man she had known for years.

"Femi slept with Keisha, that doesn't sound like a big deal to me," Maria said cautiously knowing that Zeke is now intoxicated.

Zeke half-smiled, "you are right, my friend fucked my sister, that is not a big deal, I wish it had ended there but that wasn't the case. Keisha kept coming back every other week and would meet with Femi when she could and came with her friends. She got emotionally attached to him and wanted more, and didn't mind sharing him with other girls because she would get to his room and find different girls there but like you already guessed, Femi wasn't looking for a relationship. She tried to hide it from me, I didn't know she was coming to be with that murderfucker on the weekends that she came to visit me."

"You are literally describing what I am going through with Femi right now, I still don't see the problem. Did he know Keisha was your sister?" Maria interjected.

Zeke smiled, "you are beginning to get it. No, she never told him and I didn't say anything because I thought it was a one time thing. Keisha on the other hand was young and somehow found drugs and started using, her academic performance dropped, she stole from our parents to continue to feel the rush, she got depressed. My parents checked her into a rehab after months of trying to get her clean. Femi's company peaked after he got the funding he needed to take it to the next stage and then FemCo Enterprise was reborn, AI for education, every investor threw money at him. Keisha was in love with a demon that everyone loved and worshiped, the news of his funding made news for weeks and he had TV interviews and promotion, you couldn't escape the news of the rising FemCo, I know because I helped build FemCo and for the interviews Femi couldn't attend, I did."

Zeke picked up his drink, stood up, whistled Amy Winehouse's Back to Black and sipped his drink as he walked to the side of the window in his apartment as Maria's eyes followed him. She was shocked, mixed emotions and didn't have anything to say yet.

 "I went to the rehab to see my sister, I had just finished some of the interviews for FemCo, which aired on TV and wanted to go share the good news with her, in case she had not been watching. When I got there I was told Keisha tried to kill herself, and no one could provide me with a simple reason why she would want to do that to herself after all she was getting better, talking, and feeling better. She was participating in group activities. She had cut herself with a table knife Maria, her meals were served in paper plates, including cutlery set. When I was finally able to see her, she had bandages on both wrists, her room and bathroom had no mirrors, glasses or anything she could use to hurt herself. She was happy to see me and tried to be her bubbly self but she was a shadow of herself Maria."

"I saw you on TV big shot," She said sitting up.

"That doesn't matter right now," I responded.

 "Yes, it does, I didn't know you worked with Femi," Keisha inquired.

"I do, that is my friend," I said to her.

"Keisha sobbed hearing those words from my mouth, I didn't understand at first, I knew she messed around with him that one time and chose to forget it, to save us both the embarrassment, if I had brought it up then I would have had to cut off Femi and wouldn't have been able to stay on top of things with Femi and Keisha but I missed it. Keisha played into the hands of the demon himself, she fell for the demon. Imagine if I was not in the picture," Zeke paused, and sipped his drink.

"I am sorry, I am so sorry," she said continuously as she reached out for a hug.

"You didn't do anything wrong, let's focus on getting you better and out of here," I responded feeling helpless. I didn't know how to save my sister.

"Promise you will forgive me, promise me," she asked.

"I promise, I forgive you already. Whatever it is I forgive you," I replied, holding her tight in my arms.

Zeke looked at his glass and downed the rest of the drink. Maria still amused and had no words, as her eyes followed him.

Zeke kept looking outside, looking into the sky, it was like he could see Keisha's face in the clouds.

"You promise! You promise!" she continued to ask for assurance. I pulled away from her for a bit, looked her in the eyes and reassured her that "I promise."

After a momentary silence, Keisha said "I am so sorry, I don't want to ruin this for you. I slept with Femi and continued to sleep with him every time I came to see you in the dorm before you guys finally found your apartments."

"If that's it, I forgive you. Don't even worry about it," I said.

"Let me finish Zeke," She responded.

"Sorry, go ahead," I said.

She then disclosed everything I told you, when it started, how it started, how he didn't want her the way she wanted him and how she did everything she could to get his attention. She went further saying how Femi would have sex with her and other girls and ignored her after. How she started doing drugs with one of the girls and how that got her here.

She pulled my hands and said "Can I ask you for a favor?"

"Anything, name it! Anything and you got it," I responded, my eyes were filled with tears and my face flushed with anger but somehow I was able to sprinkle a smile for my Kiki.

"Can you forgive Femi, it wasn't his fault. I fell in love with a demon and I got burnt," Keisha said.

Tears rolled down my face and soaked my shirt. I could barely speak, so I nodded.

"Please forgive, Femi, it is not his fault," she repeated, before she gave me a hug and whispered, "thank you! You are the best brother a girl can ask for."

Even in her weakest and saddest time, she still knew how to cheer me up.

Keisha killed herself two weeks after she told me everything. She had cut her wrist with the handle of the dresser in the bathroom.

Zeke downed his glass one more time, trying to keep his cool but obviously flushed, Maria could only watch with her eyes and mouth wide open.

"The shock of Keisha's death, that traumatic experience resulted in my mom having difficulty in speaking or understanding, numbness on one side of her body, and loss of vision on the same side. She was rendered helpless, her marriage fucked up, she can't hear or barely recognize me. My own mother, Maria," Zeke paused to pour himself another drink.

"I keep hearing Keisha's voice in my head, "forgive Femi, please forgive him," I probably would have forgave him but not anymore, not after this, not after making my mother a fucking vegetable," Zeke snorted, cleaned his teary eyes and said, "here is what you are going to do for me, as you can tell, I have nothing else to lose."

Zeke shared the plan with Maria.

Zeke's gaze was unwavering, his determination clear. "Will you help me, Maria? Will you be a part of this?"

Maria, still reeling from Zeke's revelations, felt a deep sense of entrapment. She was conflicted, torn between her growing feelings for Femi and the heavy burden of her own secret. Zeke's assurance that her secret was safe with him offered little comfort. "Fine, I'll help you," she said with evident reluctance. "But you have to help me win him over."

Zeke's response was a sly grin. "You got it, Maria. There is nothing I want more than to see that man pay for what he did to my family and his sins."

As they spoke, Maria's phone buzzed with a text from me. "Speak of the devil himself," she muttered, glancing at the message. "I have to go. He might want to video call me soon, and I don't want him to find me here," she said, standing up and walking slowly to the door, her mind a whirlwind of emotions.

Once inside her car, Maria sat motionless, trying to steady her shaking hands. The gravity of the situation was overwhelming. Memories of Keisha, the joyful times they shared, compared with her intimate moments with Femi, flooded her thoughts. "What am I going to do?" she whispered to herself, staring blankly into space.

Meanwhile, back in his apartment, Zeke couldn't contain his excitement as he called his father, James Walters. "Dad, she's in," he announced triumphantly.

James' voice, deep and satisfied, came through the phone. "Good job, son. You're making me proud."

"We'll make Femi pay for his sins in no time," Zeke replied, smirking.

His father's cautionary words were a stark reminder. "Just remember, we need to be careful. No mistakes," James warned.

"I know, Dad. We'll be careful," Zeke assured him confidently before ending the call.

But as Zeke set down his phone, a chilling sensation crept over him. He had felt the presence of someone lurking, and now, hearing his door lock from the outside, his heart raced with fear.

"Who's there?" Zeke called out, his voice betraying his fear. Silence was his only answer, yet the sensation of being watched was palpable.

He rushed to the door but found no one. The empty hallway and the stillness of the elevator door only deepened his unease.

The silence and emptiness of the apartment hall left Zeke with more questions than answers. Who had been watching him, and why? The unsettling feeling lingered, a foreboding sense that his plans, though seemingly on track, were under unseen scrutiny.

As Zeke stood there, the weight of his father's warning echoed in his mind, a stark reminder of the delicate balance of their vengeful plot. Unbeknownst to him, the path to retribution was becoming more treacherous, and the shadows of their scheme were drawing closer, threatening to engulf them all in a game far more dangerous than they had anticipated.

***

Maria had gone back to the apartment to ask Zeke questions she had thought about while trying to gather herself in her car.

"His dad is in on it, Fuck! Fuck!" Maria hit her hands on the steering wheels before finally driving off.

Chapter Six

"Make Money, Make Enemies."

Zeke arrived at the office early the next day, feeling uneasy after the incident at his apartment. He kept looking over his shoulder, wondering if anyone was watching him. As he walked past my office, he noticed a new person sitting at the desk outside the door.

"Who's that?" he asked one of his colleagues, nodding in the direction of the person.

"That's Femi's new personal assistant," the colleague replied. "I heard she's really good."

Zeke nodded absentmindedly and continued walking, but he couldn't shake the feeling of being watched. He arrived at his own office and sat down at his desk, trying to focus on his work. But every time he looked up, he saw me walking around, talking to my employees, and he wondered if I was the one behind the incident at his apartment.

After a few hours, Zeke decided to take a break and went to the break room to get some coffee. As he was pouring the coffee, he heard someone come in behind him. He turned around and saw me standing there, holding a file.

"Morning, Zeke," I said cheerfully. "How are you doing today?"

Zeke tried to act casual, but he was still feeling uneasy. "I'm good," he said. "Just trying to get some work done."

I nodded. "Well, I hope you're not too busy to come to the meeting this afternoon. We have some important things to discuss."

Zeke forced a smile. "Of course, I'll be there."

I nodded again and turned to leave, but then he paused and looked back at Zeke. "Is everything okay, Zeke? You seem a little...off today."

Zeke hesitated, wondering if he should tell Femi about the incident at his apartment. But then he thought better of it and shook his head. "No, I'm fine. Just a little distracted."

"You've finally gotten one of these Bay area girls distracting you, right?"
I asked, shook my head and left the break room, but Zeke couldn't shake the feeling that I was somehow involved in what had happened to him. He decided to

keep an eye on me and my new personal assistant, hoping to find some answers.

Zeke returned to his desk and tried to focus on his work, but he kept glancing up at my office. He wondered if the new personal assistant was watching him or if I had hired her to keep tabs on him. He couldn't help but feel paranoid, and it was affecting his productivity.

As the day went on, Zeke noticed that the personal assistant was constantly busy, answering phone calls, taking messages, and scheduling appointments. She seemed efficient and organized, but Zeke couldn't shake the feeling that there was more to her than met the eye.

Finally, it was time for the meeting. Zeke gathered his notes and headed to the conference room, where the personal assistant and I were already seated. Zeke took a seat, with another colleague at the opposite end of the table and tried to act casual.

"Good afternoon, everyone," I said, smiling. "I'm glad you could make it today. We have a lot to cover, so let's get started. Meet Trisha, she started today as my Personal Assistant and reports to me."

"Hi Trisha, Welcome to the team," the room echoed.

"Our sales numbers for the third quarter doubled from the second quarter, which is a great boost for the last quarter, good work, team," I said as he turned from the presentation being displayed to join the room in clapping.

Zeke tried to pay attention to the meeting, but his mind kept drifting. He couldn't help but wonder if the personal assistant was secretly working for me, spying on him and reporting back on his every move.

After the meeting, Zeke decided to take matters into his own hands. He waited until the personal assistant was alone in the break room and approached her.

"Excuse me," he said, trying to sound casual. "I couldn't help but notice how busy you've been today. You seem really good at your job."

The personal assistant smiled. "Thank you. I take pride in my work."

Zeke hesitated for a moment before deciding to take a chance. "Listen, I don't mean to be rude, but I have to ask. Are you spying on me? Did Femi hire you to keep tabs on me?"

The personal assistant's smile faded, and she looked at him seriously. "No, Zeke. I'm just here to do my job. I have no reason to spy on you."

Zeke felt a wave of relief wash over him. "I'm sorry, I guess I'm just a little paranoid lately. I had an incident at my apartment, and I don't know who's behind it."

The personal assistant's expression softened. "I'm sorry to hear that, Mr Walters. Is there anything I can do to help?"

Zeke hesitated for a moment before shaking his head. "No, it's okay. I'll figure it out. I will order home security cameras or something. Thanks for being honest with me."

The personal assistant nodded and left the break room, leaving Zeke to wonder who was really behind the incident at his apartment.

Zeke remained uneasy for days but also noticed I was not bothered about him but focused on our expansion plans to Europe and had gotten so busy that I needed to hire a Personal Assistant, he decided to let it go and remained vigilant after all he had bought and installed security cameras.

***

That week, in one of the evenings, I was surprised when there was a knock on my door. I have been texting Maria and Catherine and was aware that Maria was busy with work and Catherine was still in New York. I got up from the couch and walked to the door, wondering who it could be. When I opened it, I saw a young woman standing there, holding a plate with a pound cake on it.

"Hi neighbor," she said with a flirtatious smile. "I'm Andrea. My mom is Karen, your neighbor."

I didn't recognize the name nor remember meeting them. I nodded politely and said, "Hi, Andrea, nice to meet you."

"I heard you just moved in, and I wanted to welcome you to the neighborhood," Andrea said, continuing to give me a flirtatious smile.

"Yeah, thank you," I responded.

"I just wanted to come by and apologize for my mom's behavior," Andrea said, stepping closer to me. "She can be a bit uptight sometimes. But I wanted to make it up to you."

"Uptight? Uptight about what?" I asked.

"You didn't know? Karen was the one that called the cops on your party the other day. She is known to do that, all the neighbors knew she did it and I thought you did as well which was why I wanted to apologize,"

Andrea answered, twirling a strand of her blonde hair around her finger before putting it behind her ear.

"Do you apologize to every neighbor she calls the cops on?" I pressed.

"No! Of course not," Andrea responded as she looked at me trying to mesmerize me with her tantalizing green eyes.

I raised an eyebrow, sensing her flirtatious approach. Andrea was in her early twenties, blonde, and undeniably beautiful, but I wasn't interested in her advances. "I appreciate the gesture," I said. "But it wasn't necessary."

Andrea pouted. "Are you sure? The pound cake is really good. I made it myself. There are other things you could be pounding."

I sighed inwardly, knowing that I wasn't going to be able to get rid of her easily. I decided to take the cake and put an end to the visit. "Thank you, Andrea," I said, taking the plate from her. "I appreciate it. But I have some work to do."

Andrea's smile faded a little, but she took the hint and said goodbye, walking back to her house. I closed the door and put the plate of pound cake on the kitchen counter. I wasn't sure what to make of Andrea's visit, but I had a feeling that it wasn't the last time I would see her.

***

I arrived at the office early on Friday morning, feeling a sense of excitement in the air. The sun was just starting to rise over the San Francisco Bay, casting a golden glow over the city. It was a crisp, clear morning in mid-October, with a hint of autumn chill in the air.

As I walked into the building, I could feel the buzz of anticipation among my colleagues. I knew that today was going to be a big day - the day we would find out whether my company had won the contract with a top educational institution in the UK.

I made my way to my office, greeted my team members, who were already hard at work preparing for the big announcement. I could feel the excitement building inside me as I checked my emails and reviewed my notes one last time.

As the morning wore on, the tension in the office grew. I could feel the nerves and excitement in the air, as everyone eagerly awaited the announcement. I checked my watch every few minutes, counting down the seconds until the news would arrive.

And then, just after lunchtime, it came. My phone buzzed with an email notification, and I quickly opened it to read the news. My team had won the contract with the educational institution, beating out several other top companies.

I let out a whoop of joy and immediately jumped out of my chair, high-fiving my team members and hugging them in celebration. The excitement in the office was palpable as everyone congratulated each other and celebrated their hard work paying off.

Outside, the sun shone brighter than ever, and I couldn't help but feel a sense of gratitude and appreciation for the beauty of the moment. I knew that this was just the beginning of bigger things to come for my team and company.

My team had been working on this deal for months, and finally, they had closed it successfully. They had managed to convince the top educational institution in the UK to partner with FemCo to provide online education services with their integrated artificial intelligence. The deal was worth millions of dollars, and my team and I were thrilled.

As soon as the news broke, the entire office erupted in cheers and applause. Zeke, who had been working at his desk, heard the commotion and went to investigate. When he saw my team and I celebrating, he couldn't help but feel a twinge of jealousy. He wished that he was a part of a team that achieved such a significant milestone.

I noticed Zeke standing at the doorway and called him over. "Zeke, come and join us! We just closed the deal with the top educational institution in the UK."

Zeke's face lit up with excitement. "That's incredible! Congratulations, Femi."

I smiled. "Thanks, Zeke. It's been a lot of hard work, but it's all paid off. We're going to celebrate tonight. You should join us."

Zeke hesitated for a moment, wondering if he would be intruding on their celebration. But I insisted, and eventually, Zeke agreed to join them.

That evening, my team and I went out to a fancy restaurant to celebrate our success. Zeke tagged along, feeling like he was a part of something special. As we sat down at the table, I raised a toast to my team.

"I couldn't have done this without each and every one of you," I said, looking around the table. "We've worked hard, and now we get to reap the rewards. Cheers!"

They all clinked their glasses and took a sip of their drinks. The rest of the night was filled with laughter, good food, and lots of celebrating. Zeke felt grateful for the opportunity to be a part of the celebration, and he couldn't help but feel a newfound respect for my team and I.

***

As Maria arrived at my house, I greeted her with a smile and a bottle of champagne. We sat down on the couch, clinking our glasses in celebration.

I had texted her and Catherine earlier and told them about the new big deal my team just signed.

"I'm so proud of you," Maria said, leaning over to give me a kiss.

I smiled, feeling grateful for her support. "I couldn't have done it without my team," I said. "But it feels good to have closed such a big deal."

As we continued to sip champagne, I couldn't help but feel grateful for Maria's presence in my life. She brought a sense of happiness and calmness to my otherwise hectic schedule.

"I have to admit, I was a little nervous about telling you about the deal," I confessed. "But I knew you would be happy for me."

Maria laughed. "Of course I'm happy for you," she said. "You work so hard, and you deserve all the success you've achieved."

Maria brought out her phone from her bag, connected to the speaker, played one of the songs that she knew I enjoyed and would dance to.

"Come on, don't leave me hanging now," she said as she offered her hands to pull me up from the couch, we danced the night away, doing funny dance moves, both tipsy as we were done with our second bottle of champagne for the night.

I tried to top up my glass and realized there was no more champagne.

"Another one!" Maria said excitingly, as she walked to the wine fridge.

As the night progressed, we ended up in my bedroom, lost in each other's embrace.

"I've been looking forward to this part of the night," a tipsy Maria declared in my arms.

"You have?" I asked as I turned to her.

"Yes. Just us, here, me in your arms, is where I love being," Maria said as her eyes twinkled.

I was fully turned on, got up on my shoulder, pulled her closer, we shared a long passionate kiss, embracing and touching each other's body.

After some minutes of foreplay, I tried to reach into my bed drawer, to pick a condom.

"Not tonight, my King, I want to feel you inside of me," Maria said as she pulled me back to her and guided me in her vagina.

It was a night of celebration, both for my achievements at work and our personal connection. I couldn't help but feel grateful for Maria's presence in my life, as we fell asleep in each other's arms.

***

The morning after the celebration, Maria and I lay entwined in each other's arms, watching the sunrise through the window. The sky was painted in shades of pink and orange, the clouds resembling a watercolor painting.

Maria shifted slightly, her head resting on my chest. "I could get used to this," she said softly.

I smiled and kissed her forehead. "Me too," I replied.

As the sun continued to rise, we reluctantly got out of bed and went to the kitchen to make coffee. I brewed a fresh pot, while Maria rummaged through my fridge for breakfast ingredients.

We sat at the kitchen table, sipping coffee and munching on toast and eggs, enjoying each other's company. The morning was peaceful and quiet, with only the sound of birds chirping outside.

I couldn't help but feel content and happy. That was how I felt every time I was with Maria. The deal my company had closed the day before was a huge success, and I had celebrated with the woman I was falling in love with.

As we finished our breakfast, I took Maria's hand and pulled her towards me. "Let's go for a walk," I suggested.

Maria smiled and nodded. "I'd like that," she said.

We put on our shoes and walked out of the house, holding hands. The sun was shining brightly now, casting a warm glow on everything around them.

As we walked through the neighborhood, I felt grateful for that moment of peace and happiness. I took Maria through the same path I'd run with Catherine. I was missing her but this would do for the moment.

Maria was lost in thought, she had tried to ignore me as much as she could because she didn't know what to do. She knew she didn't want to end up in jail, and knew she couldn't hurt me, so she drank so much last night to distract herself from the inevitable.

"I have to find a way to help Zeke, without hurting Femi," she thought to herself as we walked back.

"A penny for your thoughts?" I asked.
"Penny? I can't spend that, I need dollars, Mister, I just closed a big deal, Mr get shit done, Mr. Big Banks, Mr. International," Maria said jokingly, acting goofy as ever.

"We both laughed!"

"Get in the house with your goofy self," I said as I opened the door, and spanked Maria's ass as she walked past me.

As Maria walked upstairs, she got an email and text asking her to come back to work for the afternoon shift, she ran back downstairs to share the sad news with me.

"I wish I could spend the day with you but I was just asked to come back to work," Maria said, sobbing and holding her arms around me.

"You can't call off work?" I asked.

"I did last night, which was how I was able to come here," She pulled away a little and looked into my eyes.

"Ok, I get it. I am going to miss you," I said, kissing her forehead.

Maria slowly walked back upstairs to shower and get ready to leave for work. She had noticed that the bracelet from the housewarming party was no longer on the dresser which made her smile as she walked into the bathroom.

"Do you want me to join you?" I inquired from the bedroom.

"Yes, but I know you. I am going to be late. I don't want to be late babe, " Maria said as she continued to shower.

"It's going to be quick," I tried to convince her.

"Nothing about you down there is quick," Maria rinsed her face and peeped to see where I was.

I shook my head, went to lay in bed. Maria soon got out of the shower and I watched as she got dressed. I couldn't help but smile as I watched her move around the room, getting ready for her day.

As Maria finished getting dressed, she turned to me and kissed goodbye. "Thank you for an amazing night," she said, before heading downstairs and out the door.

I watched her leave, feeling unsatisfied and wanting more of her.

Later that evening, I was at home, lounging on the couch, flipping through TV channels when I heard a knock on the door. I looked through the peephole and saw Andrea standing outside, holding a bottle of champagne and wearing a revealing dress.

Despite feeling hesitant about seeing her again after our previous encounter, I decided to let her in.

"Hey, Femi," Andrea said, her voice dripping with flirtation as she entered his house.

"Sorry to drop by unannounced, but I just wanted to come by and apologize for my mom calling the cops on you during your party. I hope you can forgive her."

Andrea walked past me, swaying her hips in a seductive way. I couldn't help but notice the way her dress hugged her curves, showing off her body.

I nodded, captivated by her body, I calmed myself down, shook my head, knowing how it will end. "I appreciate you coming over to apologize. I had forgiven her when you mentioned it the other night, and speaking of the other night, I apologize for my behavior I had a lot going on that night."

"I understand, I could be a handful sometimes," Andrea said, adjusting her dress.

Andrea walked around my house in admiration, taking in every detail. "Wow, Femi, your house is amazing!" she exclaimed. "I've always wondered what the inside looked like. The old neighbors were never really friendly, so I never got a chance to see it."

I smiled politely. "Thank you, Andrea. I'm glad you like it."

Andrea continued to explore the house, her eyes wide with wonder. She ran her hands over the smooth, polished surfaces of the marble countertops in the kitchen, and admired the antique furniture in the living room.

"This is beautiful," she said, running her fingers over the intricately carved legs of a wooden coffee table. "Is it an antique?"

I nodded. "Yes, it's been in my family for generations."

Andrea nodded, clearly impressed. "You have such good taste, Femi. I wish I had a house like this."

I chuckled. "Well, you never know, Andrea. Maybe someday you will."

Andrea smiled at me, then turned to look out the window. "This view is amazing. You can see the entire city from up here."

I nodded. "Yes, it's one of the reasons I bought this house."

"Can I see upstairs?" Andrea asked.

I declined. "Let's drink the champagne you brought," I redirected.

We sat on the couch, sipping champagne, and talking about work and life. I found himself enjoying

Andrea's company, and the champagne seemed to be doing its job, making me feel more relaxed and carefree.

Andrea, not letting go, turned to face him, her eyes bright with excitement, smiled, eyeing me up and down. "I also wanted to thank you for the show you put on with your girlfriend last night. I saw you guys through the window, and I have to say, I don't mind sharing."

I raised an eyebrow, feeling a mix of confusion and discomfort at Andrea's statement. "I'm sorry, what do you mean?"

Andrea chuckled. "Oh, come on, Femi. You don't have to play dumb. I saw you and your girlfriend last night. I don't mind joining in if you're interested or just coming by to get a piece of that huge dick of yours, when she is not here."

I shook my head, feeling excited at Andrea's forwardness. I realized that I didn't close the blinds. My night with Maria, flashed in my memory for a second, wondering what Andrea must have seen. "You want to see where all that action took place?"

Andrea's face lit up hearing me ask. "Yeah. Yes, please." She downed her drink and grabbed on to the hand that I offered.

I led her up the stairs, holding my glass of champagne in the other hand.

"Welcome to the lion's den," I said.

My bedroom was a sanctuary of comfort and luxury, with tall open windows that allowed a gentle breeze to flow in. The room was tastefully decorated with dark wood furniture, plush bedding, and soft lighting that created a cozy and inviting atmosphere. The walls were painted a soothing shade, which added to the peacefulness of the space.

The tall open windows were the main feature of the room, offering a stunning view of the city lights and allowing a cool breeze to flow in. The curtains were made of soft white fabric, billowing gently in the breeze, adding to the romantic ambiance of the room.

The bed was the centerpiece of the room, with a high headboard made of dark wood and soft white bedding that looked inviting and comfortable. A few throw pillows were scattered on the bed, adding to the cozy feel of the space. On either side of the bed, there were matching nightstands with small lamps that cast a warm glow over the room.

Andrea looked around in awe, turned and walked towards Femi who was trying to close the blinds.

"Leave it open, I don't care if anyone is watching," Andrea smiled and stepped closer to me.

She got so close, and placed her hand on my crotch, rubbing it, slowly before bringing out my dick.

"What are you doing?" I said softly as I watched her go down on her knees.

Andrea smiled, on her knees as she watched me sip my drink, facing the open window.

"Like that, yes." I moaned softly, giving her directions on how to please me.

I adjusted my body as Andrea continued to go down on me, because I had seen Karen from my opened window and had caught her looking up, I had a devilish smile on my face.

Karen sensed something was off from her house across the street, she saw blonde hair and with that smirk on my face, it could be Andrea. She looked for her phone, called Andrea's number but she wasn't picking up. She walked to her bedroom where she could only see blonde hair around my pubic area.

I noticed that Karen was back and decided to give her a show, acting like I enjoyed it more than I did. I downed my drink, dropped the glass on the floor and placed my hand on the window.

An obviously pissed Karen kept calling her daughter hoping she wasn't the one performing the sexual act she was witnessing in my room from Andrea's room. She went downstairs to her garage and found Andrea's car there.

"Oh my god! Oh my god! It better not be here," Karen said to herself.

She walked back into the house, picked up and dialed her friend whom she knows has a daughter who is friends with Andrea.

Phone rang twice, Karen couldn't wait to talk, no pleasantries, "Suzie, is Andrea there?".

"I don't think so," Suzie responded.

"Are you sure? Maybe she is with Lucy?" Karen pressed.

"No, Lucy is here with me. Is everything ok?" Suzie asked.

"Yeah, I just need her to do something real quick that's all. Thank you though," Karen said, cutting the call.

Now fully flushed, a distraught Karen heads back to Andrea's room, her mind filled with hatred.

I was in a different position, Karen could see me in what looked like a doggy position, she couldn't see the face of the girl, she could see it's a white girl's body and I was thrusting back and forth.

I had turned back slightly and had caught a glimpse of Karen watching, I continued to thrust harder and spanked Andrea.

Andrea had no idea what was going on, she was letting out screams of pleasure, moaning louder more than she had ever let out.

Karen couldn't risk calling the cops, the neighbors would see her daughter come out of my house, which would be disgraceful and cause her more humiliation and hurt.

Andrea, still lost in the land of pleasure I provided her, and was following all the directions I was given her.

I knew I was close, I put my tongue out, turned Andrea close to the window, pulled out my dick and burst cum in her mouth with splash on her face as I climaxed.

Uncontrollable tears rolled out of Karen's eyes as she watched her daughter lost on my pipe of happiness, unbothered and pleasured.

As my drip of semens slowed down.

"Oh shit! Oh shit!" Andrea finally opened her eyes, saw her mother from her house. She quickly rushed away from the window, looked for her dress, shoes and rushed downstairs to go home.

The show was over and I closed the curtains.

I went downstairs, closed my door, showered and called it a night.

This was now personal for both Karen and I.

Chapter Seven

I avoided Karen in any way I could knowing that I now had the upper hand after the incident from the night, Karen watched me from Andrea's room being pleasured by her daughter.

Karen now outrightly stalks me and watches my every move, she knows everyone that comes to my house, the time I leave for work in the morning, the time I return, the times I go running and the time I go to bed.

Karen felt she failed herself by not paying attention to her daughter, "How could I have missed this?" she said as she watched me drive my luxury car into my driveway.

***

I woke up early one morning, feeling energized and ready to start the day. I took a quick shower, got dressed, and grabbed my keys to head out to the office. As I walked out of my house and got into my car, I had a strange feeling that someone was watching him.

Looked around, I saw Karen standing on her porch, watching me with a stern expression on her face. I ignored her and drove off, but I couldn't shake off the feeling that she was still watching me.

The drive to the office was uneventful as I vibed to my afrobeats playlist, but I couldn't help but feel uneasy. I checked my mirrors several times, half-expecting to see Karen's car following me. I tried to brush it off, thinking that it was just my imagination playing tricks on me.

As I pulled into the parking lot of the company, I noticed a car that looked similar to Karen's parked a few spaces away. I couldn't tell if it was hers, but the sight of the car made me feel even more uncomfortable.

I got out of the car and walked towards the entrance of the building, trying my best to keep my composure. However, I couldn't help but feel like I was being watched. I turned around and saw Karen's car driving slowly past the building.

I took a deep breath and tried to shake off the feeling of being watched. I entered the building and went straight to my office, hoping to forget about the strange encounter.

***

I was sitting at my desk in my office, when I picked up my phone to call Cody.

"Hey man, what's up?" Cody answered on the second ring.

"Not much, just wanted to catch up," I said with a smile. "How have you been?"

"I've been good," Cody replied. "How about you? How's the company doing?"

"We just closed a deal with a top educational institution in the UK," I said, my excitement palpable. "It's going to be huge for us."

"Wow, that's amazing," Cody said, impressed. "Congrats, man."

"Thanks. Speaking of the company, I wanted to offer you a position," I said. "I need someone to head up our customer success team, and I think your background would be a perfect fit."

"Really?" Cody asked, surprised. "I'd love that, man. When do I start?"

"As soon as you can. We're growing quickly, and I could use the help," I said. "I'll send you the details of the position and the benefits package. We talked about this at Saint Tropez"

"Thanks, Femi. I appreciate it," Cody said, his excitement growing. "This is going to be great."

"I'm looking forward to having you on board," I said. "You should come down to the office and check it out. We can grab lunch."

"That sounds good," Cody replied. "I'll see you there."

I hung up the phone, feeling good about the decision to bring Cody on board. I was sure that he would be an asset to the company and help us continue to grow.

As I leaned back in my chair, I thought about the future of FemCo and all the possibilities that lay ahead.

After a long day at the office, I decided to tell Zeke about my decision to hire Cody.

"Hey man, can we talk for a second?" I asked as I approached Zeke's desk.

"Yeah, sure. What's up?" Zeke replied, looking up from his computer.

"I wanted to tell you that I've decided to hire Cody for the head of customer success position," I said.

"Really? That's awesome news, man! Cody is great at what he does. I'm sure he'll do a fantastic job here as well," Zeke said with a smile.

"I'm really excited to have him on board. I think he'll be a great addition to the team," I replied.

"Definitely. We should celebrate. How about we grab a drink after work?" Zeke suggested.

"Sounds good to me. Let's do it," I agreed.

After finishing up our work, Zeke and I headed to a nearby bar to celebrate.

Zeke and I sat at the bar, enjoying our drinks as we chatted about work.

We ordered a round of drinks and raised their glasses to Cody and the success of their company.

As if on cue, the door to the bar swung open, and Cody walked in. I waved him over to our table, and Cody made his way over, grinning from ear to ear.

"Hey guys, mind if I join you?" Cody asked.

"Of course not," I said, pulling out a chair for him.

Zeke raised his glass in a toast. "Congratulations, welcome to the team, Cody! Here's to the start of a new adventure!"

We clinked our glasses together, and I couldn't help but feel grateful for my friends and the success of my company.

After a few rounds of drinks, I brought up the topic of my upcoming trip to London.

"Guys, I'm excited about this trip to London. I'll be expanding our deal with the educational institution there," I said.

"That deal is huge for us! When are you going?" Zeke asked.

"In two weeks. And the good news is, I won't be leaving the company unattended. I've got you two," I replied.

"Welcome onboard again, Cody. I can't wait for you to start," Zeke said, clinking his glass with Cody's.

"Thanks, man! I'm excited to join the team and make an impact," Cody replied.

"Now, if anything comes up and you can't reach me, don't worry. My personal assistant will be available to handle anything you need," I added.

Zeke and Cody nodded in agreement, and I raised my glass for a toast.

"Here's to expanding our horizons and taking our company to the next level!"

A heavy vibration sound buzzed while they were sipping their drinks.

I took out my phone and saw a message from Catherine. He smiled as he read it. "Hey, it's been a while since we spent some quality time together. I'm free this weekend. Want to grab lunch?"

I quickly replied, "Yes, let's do it. How about Saturday?"

Catherine replied, "Sounds perfect. How about noon at that Italian place we went to on our first date?"

My heart skipped a beat at the mention of our first date. It seemed like ages ago, but the memories of that night were still fresh in my mind. I replied, "Perfect. I'll see you there at noon."

After being lost in my own world, "I am glad we were able to do this and make it happen," I said, raising my head back up, my phone back in my pocket.

We called it a night and all left for our cars.

***

"Was that you texting him?" Zeke asked through text.

Maria was with a patient when her phone beeped. "I didn't text him, I am at work," she responded.

"That was probably Catherine then, because we wrapped up as soon as he got a series of messages on his phone," Zeke responded, sitting in his car as he watched Cody and I drive off.

"You don't seem to be taking me seriously," Zeke texted again after waiting for a few minutes without a response from Maria.

"It seems like that person really wants to talk to you," the patient said jokingly.

Maria knew it was Zeke, she tried to gather herself and finish administering medication for the patient.

"This should help relieve the pain some more," smiled as she responded to the patient.

"I do take you seriously, I was with him last week, I can't impose myself a lot on him, I will lose him and we don't want that. Do we?" Maria finally replied.

"For your sake, you better not lose him. He is going to London in two weeks, get preggy for him asap," an agitated Zeke responded.

"I know, I promise I am on it," Maria hit the send button, put her phone back in her pocket and smiled at her next patient.

Zeke sent her a thumbs up and finally drove off.

***

However, throughout the day, I couldn't help but feel like Karen was still watching me, even though I couldn't see her.

As I drove toward my house, I saw her standing on her porch. It was like she was expecting me, she had a cup of tea in her hands with a blank stare.

I had a grin on my face as my afrobeats playlist continued to play, I pulled into my driveway.

"Hi Karen, How's Andrea?" I said before picking up my laptop bag.

Karen had no response, she sipped her cup of tea, staring blank toward me.

"Tell her I miss her," I laughed as I walked, opened the door of the house and got in.

I got upstairs to my room and saw Karen standing in Andrea's her room with the same cup of team.

"Wetin dey do this woman? This woman don dey craze o!" I closed my curtains, dropped my bag, showered and retired for the night.

***

The next day, I met up with Catherine at the Italian restaurant.

Catherine arrived late lunch wearing a form-fitting sweater dress in a deep shade of burgundy that hugged her curves in all the right places. The long sleeves and high neckline were perfect for the cool November weather in Oakland, and the dress ended just above her knees, showing off her toned legs. She paired the dress with black knee-high boots with a slight heel, which added a touch of elegance to the outfit. Her hair was styled in loose waves that cascaded down her back, and her makeup was simple but flawlessly applied. As I greeted her, I couldn't help but stare at her with admiration, and Catherine's smile showed she knew the effect she had on me.

We hugged and kissed each other on the cheeks.

"It's so good to see you," I said.

"It's good to see you too," Catherine replied, smiling.

We sat down at a table and ordered some food. As we ate, we talked about everything that had happened since Catherine's return from New York.

"I've missed you so much," Catherine said.

"I've missed you too," I replied.

After we finished eating, I suggested we take a walk in the park nearby. Catherine agreed, and we headed out.

As we walked, I put my arm around Catherine's waist, and she leaned her head on my shoulder.

"I'm so glad we're doing this," Catherine said.

"Me too," I replied. "I've been so busy lately, I've hardly had time to catch my breath."

Catherine nodded. "I know how that feels. Work has been crazy for me too."

We walked in silence for a few moments, just enjoying each other's company. Then Catherine spoke up again.

"Femi, I know we haven't talked about this in a while, but where do you see us going?"

I took a deep breath. I knew this conversation was coming, but I still wasn't sure how to answer. "Honestly, Catherine, I'm not sure. I like you a lot, but I'm not sure if I'm ready for anything serious right now."

Catherine nodded. "I understand. I just wanted to make sure we were on the same page."

I smiled. "We are. And I promise, I'll keep you in the loop about where my head's at."

Catherine smiled back. "Thanks, Femi. That means a lot."

We continued walking, enjoying the cool breeze and the sound of the leaves rustling. I was happy to be spending time with Catherine again.
"So, I have some news," I said, breaking the silence. "I'm going to London next week."

"London?" Catherine asked, surprised. "For work?"

"Yeah," I replied. "The deal we closed that I mentioned to you is with a big company over there, and I need to go for our expansion. I'll be gone for a few days."

Catherine looked up at him, a small frown on her face. "That's too bad. I was hoping we could spend more time together."

I smiled down at her. "We still have a few days before I leave. How about I come over to your place tonight?"

Catherine's face lit up. "That sounds perfect. Just promise me you won't sneak out this time."

I chuckled. "I promise. I'll stay as long as you want me to."

We continued walking, enjoying each other's company as we chatted about our plans for the night at Catherines'. The park was crowded with people, but

we found a quiet bench near a small pond and sat
down to enjoy the view.

As we watched the ducks swimming in the pond, I
couldn't help but stare at Catherine. The tight-fitting
deep shade of burgundy dress hugged her curves in
all the right places as she sat beside me. Her hair
which was in loose waves, framed her face perfectly,
and her eyes sparkled in the sunlight.

"You look stunning," I said, unable to resist the
compliment.

Catherine blushed, looking away. "Oh, stop it. You're
making me blush."

I smiled, enjoying the way she reacted to my words.
We sat in silence for a few minutes, enjoying the peace
and quiet of the park.

"I'm serious, you look stunning. Like, look at you," I
said, my hands expressive.

Catherine, still blushing, and now shy, stood up
heading away from the crowd, I stood up, caught up
with her, and put my arm around her shoulder.

"You are something else, you know?" She turned to
me, all smiles.

"You bring this guy out, I don't recognize him, but he comes out when I am with you," I confessed.

"I like him, I want him around more," Catherine responded.

"See you in a bit," I said as I held the door for Catherine to get into her car. I kissed her and closed the door and watched her drive off.

***

As I knocked on Catherine's door, I took a deep breath, trying to calm my racing heart. When Catherine opened the door, I couldn't help but stare at her. She was wearing a black lacy lingerie set, which left little to the imagination.

"Wow," I said, my eyes still fixed on Catherine's body. "You look incredible."

Catherine smiled and motioned for him to come inside. "Thank you," she said, closing the door behind him. "I wasn't sure you were actually going to show up."

"I said I would, didn't I?" I replied, holding up the bouquet of red roses I brought for her. "These are for you."

"Thank you, they're beautiful," Catherine said, taking the roses and inhaling their sweet scent.

I also handed her a bottle of wine. "I thought we could dance, drink some wine, and just enjoy each other's company."

Catherine smiled and led me to the living room, where she turned on some music. I pulled her close, and we began to sway to the music. We danced and talked for hours, sipping wine and enjoying each other's company.

As the night wore on, I found himself lost in Catherine's eyes. I leaned in to kiss her, and she met me halfway. The kiss was soft and gentle at first, but it quickly deepened into a passionate embrace.

We broke apart, gasping for breath, and I whispered, "I'm glad I came over tonight."

Catherine smiled and pulled me back in for another kiss before I could finish speaking. It deepened again but this time, she pushed me on the couch, gave me a sexy look. She bent down to pick the bottle of wine, drank from the bottle and slowly *catwalked* to me.

I was a little shaken, and happily surprised. I was seeing this side of Catherine for the first time and loved it. I licked my lips, showing that I liked what I saw and was very much interested.

Catherine slowly whined on me, showing her curves from behind, allowing her soft skin to rub on my laps. She continued to tease me slowly until I couldn't take it any longer. I pulled her by her hips on my lap, choked her, drawing her closer to me, I kissed her neck, until Catherine let go and let out a moan. I separated her legs with my hand, my hand hiked her soft thighs to a waterfall between her legs, she had no panties on, she continued to moan as I played with her. She got up when I tried to adjust myself on the couch and before I could say Catherine, I was a lollipop in her mouth, We explored each other's body and passionately made love all night on her couch, we didn't make it to the bed.

***

The morning after our passionate night, Catherine woke up early to make breakfast for me. She wore a silk robe and had her hair tied up in a messy bun. I watched her move around the kitchen, appreciating her curves and the way the fabric clung to her body.

"Good morning, sleepyhead. I hope you're hungry. I'm making pancakes and bacon," She said.

Struggling to keep my eyes opened, I said "Good morning, gorgeous. That sounds amazing. Thank you."

As we sat down to eat, I shared more details about my upcoming trip to London. She listened attentively, and when I finished, she looked at me with a mischievous grin. "You know, I wouldn't mind keeping you here with me a little longer," she confessed.

"As much as I'd love to stay, I have to go. But I promise I'll make it up to you when I get back," I responded.

As we finished breakfast, I got up to leave. I stepped outside, and as I closed the door, I saw Karen standing on the sidewalk with her dog. She looked up to make sure I saw her, and then it was obvious that she had been waiting for me.

"Lovely day, isn't it?" Karen said, looking at her dog but loud enough for me to hear her.

I got in my car and drove off, feeling uneasy. "She is definitely following me," I couldn't shake the feeling that Karen was watching me, even when I couldn't see her.

***

I arrived at London Heathrow Airport, walked towards the arrivals gate, looked around and saw my cousin Bidemi waving at me with a big smile on his face.

"Femi, my brother, welcome to London," Bidemi said as we hugged.

"Thanks, Biddy. It's good to see you," I replied.

"How was your flight?" Bidemi asked as we walked towards the car park.

"It was good. Long, but good," I answered.

Bidemi opened the trunk and placed my luggage inside before we both got into the car.

"So, how's business in Oakland?" Bidemi asked as he drove towards West London.

"It's going well. We're expanding our operations, and I just hired a new head of customer success," I answered.

"Great to hear. And what brings you to London?" Bidemi asked.

"I'm here to explore new business opportunities and expand our operations. I'll also be attending your marriage ceremony," I replied.

Bidemi smiled. "Yes, I can't wait to introduce you to my wife. You'll love her. She's mixed, white English mother and Nigerian father."

I was surprised. "Really? I thought you said you didn't want to marry a Nigerian girl."

Bidemi chuckled. "I know, I know, but she's different. You'll see."

I smiled. "I can't wait to meet her."

We arrived at Bidemi's house, and I was amazed at how beautiful it was.

"Wow, Biddy, this place is amazing," I said as we walked inside.

"Thanks, man. I worked hard to get it," Bidemi replied.

I took a seat on the couch while Bidemi went to the kitchen to grab some drinks.

"So, how's everything with you and Catherine?" Bidemi asked as he handed me a beer.

I smiled. "It's good. I really like her."

"That's great to hear. Do you like her the way you like or love Maria?" Bidemi asked.

I nodded. "Yeah, man. I like both of them, they bring out two different parts of me that I don't even know are there but I love it."

We chatted for a while before I decided to take a nap to recover from the jet lag before asking Bidemi to take me to my hotel.

"You don't want me committing my atrocities here in your soon to be marital home," I joked.

"For real, I don't want any of these London baddies thinking you live here. I don't want to go through what Sophie pulled the last time you were here before you went to school," Bidemi declared.

We both laughed!

"My guy, Sophie, was a wild one, bro! When she was done with me even after you left, I was so embarrassed, that I left to go stay with my parents. You know how I don't like living with my parents but that was a better hell than what Sophie brought to my apartment building everyday," Bidemi said as he closed the door behind him.

"You can't blame a man for being blessed down there," I said as Bidemi did the cross sign and kissed his finger.

***

We got to the hotel I was staying at, I checked in and headed to my room using the directions provided by the hotel receptionist. I opened the door to my hotel room, and Bidemi followed me inside, carrying my suitcase.

"I still can't believe you're getting married, man," I said, dropping my bags on the floor.

Bidemi chuckled. "Yeah, me neither. But it's happening, and I couldn't be happier. I can't wait for you to meet, Rebecca, my bride-to-be."

"I can't wait to meet her either," I said, walking over to the mini-bar and grabbing a bottle of water.

"Why do you have a black g-string beside your backpack? What happened on your flight?" Bidemi asked, sitting down on one of the chairs while holding the g-string with his left thumb and index fingers.

I grinned mischievously. "Let's just say I had a little bit of fun in first class."

Bidemi raised an eyebrow. "Oh yeah? What happened?"

"Well, there was this gorgeous air hostess who kept coming over to my seat, flirting with me. So, I decided to play along and see where it went," I said, taking a sip of water.

"And?" Bidemi asked, leaning forward in his seat.

"And let's just say we made our way to the bathroom and caused severe turbulence," I said, grinning.

Bidemi burst out laughing. "Man, you never change. Always the ladies' man."

I shrugged. "Hey, when you're single and good-looking, why not have some fun?"

Bidemi shook his head, still chuckling. "Well, just be careful, man. You don't want to catch anything while you're out here."

I rolled my eyes. "Don't worry, I always use protection."

"Good to know," Bidemi said, standing up. "Well, let's go out and explore London. I want to show you around before the wedding."

I nodded, putting down the water bottle. "Sounds like a plan. Lead the way, Biddy."

Chapter Eight

I woke up to the sound of my phone buzzing, groggily reached over and saw that I had several messages from Maria, Catherine, and Tessa surprisingly. I rubbed my eyes and opened up the first message.

Maria: Hey Femi, those hidden gems you posted yesterday looked amazing! Hope you're having a great time in London.

I smiled and quickly typed out a response.

"Thanks, Maria! It's been a great trip so far," I responded.

I then opened up Catherine's message.

Catherine: Hey, handsome! Those pictures you posted yesterday were stunning. Can't wait to hear all about it when you get back.

I grinned and sent a quick reply to Catherine before moving on to Tessa's message.

Tessa: Welcome to London, Femi! Would love to catch up and show you some of my favorite spots in the city. Let me know if you're free later today.

My eyes widened in surprise. I hadn't seen Tessa since after my birthday trip to Saint Tropez, but I was excited at the prospect of catching up with an old friend. I quickly responded to her message.

"Thanks, Tessa! I'd love to meet up later today. What time and where?" I responded.

After sending the message, I got up and headed to the shower, feeling energized and excited for the day ahead.

I finished taking a shower, dried off, and grabbed my phone to check for any new messages. I saw a text from Tessa with a dinner invitation for later in the evening.

Tessa: Let's do dinner tonight at 8 pm at this lovely Brazilian restaurant I know. What do you say?

I smiled to myself, happy to have another social engagement on my calendar. I replied quickly.

"Hi Tessa, that sounds great. I'm looking forward to it. See you at 8," I replied.

Just as I finished sending the text, I received another message. This time, it was from Bidemi.

Bidemi: Hey cuz, I'm downstairs. Be there in 5.

I looked out the window and saw Bidemi's car parked on the street. I quickly got dressed and headed out to meet him.

When I got in the car, Bidemi greeted me with a smile. "Hey bro, you look good, man."

"Thanks, bro. You too," I replied. "So where are we going?"

"We're heading to Rebecca's apartment, she asked me to help pick up some stuff from a store not far from the hotel you are staying at," Bidemi said. "She's having a little bridal shower get-together with her friends before they head to Barbados next week."

"Ah, okay, look at you already being a good husband," I said, nodding. "I'm excited to meet her."

Bidemi drove through the streets of London, and soon we arrived at Rebecca's apartment. As we walked in, we could hear the sound of laughter and chatter coming from one of the rooms.

Rebecca came out to greet us, looking radiant in a pink dress. "Hey, guys! Welcome!" she said, kissing and hugging Bidemi and then turning to me. "You must be Femi. Bidemi's told me so much about you."

I smiled. "Nice to finally meet you, Rebecca."

As we chatted, I couldn't help but notice the energy and excitement in the room. It was clear that Rebecca and her friends were all very close and excited about the upcoming trip.

Rebecca introduced me to her friends, Amaka and Chloe, as well as two other girls whose names I didn't catch.

I didn't catch their names because as soon as I met Amaka, I felt a sudden jolt in my heart, which made me feel helpless. I was lost in her beautiful eyes, and I couldn't take my eyes off her. I knew I had to speak up, but I was briefly tongue-tied.

"Pleasure to meet you," I finally said, and repeated the same to the other girls that I didn't catch their names.

"Is it just me or did it just get hotter here, can I get water please?" I said after meeting Rebecca's friends.

They all laughed!

"He is funny!" One of the girls said.

"I will get you water over here," Amaka said, leading the way to where the fridge was in the kitchen.

"Watch out for that one, he might be a Yoruba demon," Chloe said.

The girls chuckled. Bidemi and Rebecca in each other's arms watched as it was all unfolding in their eyes.

Amaka was wearing a stunning white dress that flowed to her knees, with a plunging neckline that showcased her cleavage. The dress was fitted at the waist, accentuating her curves, and it had a subtle slit at the side, revealing her toned legs. She wore her hair in soft curl braids, and her makeup was flawless, with a bold red lipstick that made her lips look fuller. Her overall look was breathtaking, and I couldn't stop staring at her as she gave him a cup of water.

"Thank you," was all I said as I watched her walk back to her friends.

They were all friendly and welcoming, and soon I found myself chatting and laughing with them as if we'd known each other for years.

My phone buzzed, while I was watching a football game with Bidemi, two top English football teams were playing for the third spot in the league.

"Do you have to go?" Bidemi asked.

"Not, yet Biddy. It is my personal assistant sending me a reminder and confirmation of my meetings tomorrow," I replied.

"Wait! Big man, you've got an assistant now?" Bidemi was surprised with his mouth open and now focused his attention on me.

"Yeah," I nodded.

"Oh my god, the poor girl gotta do two jobs because I'm sure you are piping her to release the pressure of her hard work," Bidemi whispered, not wanting Rebecca to hear.

"Nah! I don't mix business with pleasure," I defended myself.

"Since, when? Since when, bruv?" Bidemi cuts in.

We both laughed!

I continued, "seriously, I am not trying to lose everything because of that, I can always get that outside of work and you know, ya boy isn't lacking."

"Correct! You've been working on this project for ages. I am happy it is finally bearing fruits like you predicted." Bidemi said, feeling confident in me.

"Do you know anything about Emily Garethson?" I asked.

"The name sounds familiar, but not sure, where I know or have heard the name," Bidemi responded.

"She is the CEO of Real Edu UK," I provided more information to help refresh Biddy's memory.

"Ah! Now I know who she is. She has been in the news a lot lately here in the UK talking about how we should optimize the education system here in the UK, and about allowing children to get all the help needed to help advance the education system through artificial intelligence without tagging children lazy," Bidemi spoke passionately as he knows he will soon be a father but he and Rebecca had decided not to share the information till after the wedding.

"Interesting," I said.

"Is it your company's AI she is looking to utilize to further boost her ambition to become the next Secretary of State for Education," Bidemi asked.

"I don't know about her ambition to become the Secretary of State for Education, but yes we are currently in conversations with her team and I have a meeting with her on Wednesday," I said proudly.

"We are ready for brunch babe," Rebecca said, stepping in the frame of Bidemi.

"You look stunning, baby. Look at her looking like a freshly squeezed sweet orange juice," Bidemi praised his fiancee. "Femi, I didn't say you can look," Bidemi said, side-eyed me as he refocused on his fiancee. I shook my head, with his palm on my face thinking to himself, "the streets have lost another soldier. Gone too soon."

"Babe, doesn't Amaka work for Real Edu?" Bidemi asked.

That sprung me back to reality from my thoughts as I awaited Rebecca's answer, every second I waited for her to confirm or speak those three words, "yes she does or no she doesn't" felt like eternity.

When Rebecca finally responded, her response was far from what I was eager to hear, I was confused.

"I think so," Rebecca responded.

I thought to himself, "you think so? You think so, you don't know if your friend works there or not? Are you guys even friends? Is this one of the things where girls pick their best looking girls as bridesmaids and don't like each other, what is this?"

As Bidemi and I both attempted to get up to head downstairs to the car for brunch. Bidemi said, "She works there."

My eyebrow now fully raised, wondered how Biddy knew. "How do you know that?" I whispered.

"I think so in women's language means yes without saying it." Bidemi responded.

"What?" I exclaimed.
"One would think, with your numerous years of experience in the land of the other gender, building, remodeling and laying down pipes as the world renown plumber. You'd have taken some time off to understand their language but nope all you do is destroy and remodel the kitchen sink, like the handyman that you are," Bidemi said as he walked towards Rebecca.

"Is Femi a handyman as well?" Chloe asked, clueless of what was being discussed.

"Yes! A good one too." Bidemi responded.

"I might need your help with my kitchen sink, it drains slowly, it might be clogged," Chloe said, seeking my face for help.

Bidemi is trying so hard not to laugh, the girls didn't understand what was going on.

"I don't have the license to fix anything here in the UK, I am certified only in California, not all the states in the US. I won't want you to run into any trouble later and your insurance refuses to cover it because you hired an unlicensed handyman," I responded.

***

The brunch place in London that Bidemi, Rebecca, Chloe and I visited was a quaint little café called "The Posh Bean." It had a charming and cozy atmosphere with warm lighting, wooden tables and chairs, and vintage decor. The walls were decorated with black and white photos of London landmarks, giving the place a classic feel.

As we walked in, the aroma of freshly brewed coffee and baked goods filled the air. The café was bustling with people, chatting and sipping on their drinks. The group spotted Amaka and her friends sitting at a long table by the window, adorned with a beautiful floral centerpiece.

Amaka was wearing a stunning off-the-shoulder dress in a vibrant shade of red, complementing her smooth, dark skin. The dress hugged her curves in all the right places, and she paired it with strappy black heels. Her hair was styled in a sleek, low ponytail, and she wore minimal jewelry, letting the dress speak for itself. I couldn't help but admire her from afar as we made our way to the table.

While we were eating and drinking bottomless mimosas, Bidemi turned to Amaka and said, "Hey, Amaka, don't you work at Real Edu UK?"

Amaka nodded. "Yes, I do. Why do you ask?"

Bidemi turned to me and said, "Tell her, man."

I grinned and turned to Amaka. "Well, I have a meeting with the executives of Real Edu UK on Wednesday."

Amaka's eyes widened in surprise. "Really? That's great! I work there as a project manager. Which of the executives are you meeting with?"

"Funny you should ask," I replied, "It's Emily Garethson."

Amaka's jaw dropped. "Wow, you're meeting with the CEO herself? That's amazing!"

Rebecca chimed in, "Emily is one of the most successful female CEOs in London. Real Edu UK is a fantastic company. You'll love it."

Chloe added, "And Amaka is one of the best project managers there. She's doing amazing things for the company."

Amaka smiled modestly and thanked them. "I love working at Real Edu UK. We're doing some really exciting projects."

I smiled at her. "I'm looking forward to seeing it all firsthand on Wednesday."

"His comp…," Bidemi was about to mention FemCo when I pinched him to stop.

After finishing our brunch, Bidemi, Rebecca, Chloe, Amaka, the girls and I stepped outside The Posh Bean, exchanging pleasantries.

"Thanks for coming, guys," Rebecca said, hugging each one of them.

"Of course, we wouldn't miss it for the world, see you next week at the airport." Chloe replied, smiling.

I turned to Rebecca, "This was fun, I am glad Biddy invited me."

Rebecca turned to Bidemi. "Biddy! It's been a while since I heard someone call him that, I am glad you were able to make it. Good luck with work here in London."

"That's good to hear," Bidemi said, glancing at me.

I leaned in close to Amaka's ear. "I can't wait to see you soon," I whispered, giving her a charming smile and a hug followed.

Amaka's cheeks turned pink as she smiled back at me. "Me too," she whispered back, while in his arms more seconds than she should for a hug.

Bidemi noticed the exchange and grinned. "Alright, guys, we better get going. Rebecca needs her beauty sleep," he said, ushering them towards his car.

As we got into the car, I couldn't stop thinking about Amaka's smile and how I was looking forward to seeing her again.

***

I stretched out on the bed, letting out a long yawn as I set down my laptop. I had been working on some emails that had piled up while I was on my way to London. My phone buzzed, checked and it was a message from Tessa with the name of the Brazilian restaurant we were meeting at. I quickly got up, washed my face, and changed clothes.

As I arrived at the restaurant, I saw Tessa sitting at a table by the window. She waved at me as I approached and grinned, feeling happy to see her again. We hugged each other, and I sat down across from her.

"Hey, you look great!" Tessa said, smiling at me.

"Thanks, you too!" I replied, feeling pleased by the compliment. "It's good to see, I didn't know you stayed in London," I said with a smile.

We quickly ordered food and drinks, and the conversation flowed smoothly. We reminisced about our time in Saint Tropez. I found himself enjoying Tessa's company more and more as the evening went on with our banters and flirting. It was Saint Tropez again but on steroids.

As we finished our meal and walked out of the restaurant, Tessa turned to me and said, "Hey, Femi, do you want to come to see my apartment? It's not too far from here."

I smiled and nodded, "Sure, I'd love to but I can't tonight."
"Are you sure? I know we just ate but I was really looking forward to that Nigerian steak," Tessa said looking at my pants, with her finger redirecting her hair strand back behind her ear while licking her lips.

I continued to smile, "you know, I can't resist you when you do that." I pulled her close, kissed her, grabbed her butt, and gave it a light spanking.

As I decline Tessa's invitation to go to her apartment, Tessa's face falls slightly, and a hint of disappointment crosses her features. However, she quickly recovered and put on a smile when I said, "I will make it up to you, I promise," I said walking towards a cab and headed back to my hotel.

***

My trip to Oxford ICT was a success. I arrived at the Oxford ICT building early in the morning and was met by the Director of Oxford ICT, who gave me a warm welcome. I was then introduced to the team members who were working on the project. They gave me a brief overview of the current process, and I asked several questions to clarify some of the issues they were having.

After the briefing, I presented my presentation on behalf of FemCo, highlighting the ways my company could help improve their process and solve their current and future challenges. I was well-prepared and confident in my delivery, and the team members were impressed by my knowledge and expertise. They asked some follow-up questions, which I answered without hesitation.

After the meeting, the Director of Oxford ICT thanked me for my time and said that they were impressed by my presentation. They told me that they were looking to kick off the project with FemCo in the new year. They appreciated me for being there in person to provide a detailed overview of what the project would look like and all possible improvements. I left the meeting feeling optimistic about the potential partnership.

Later that evening, I joined the Oxford ICT team for dinner at a local restaurant. We continued our discussion about the project and talked about other topics, such as our personal lives and interests. The atmosphere was friendly and relaxed, and I enjoyed the opportunity to get to know the team members better.

As I traveled back to London, I reflected on the day's events and felt confident that FemCo had made a good impression. I was looking forward to expanding my company in the UK and the Oxford ICT team were the first adopters and hoped that this would get FemCo's name out more in the UK and possibly expand in Europe as well.

***

I sat in his hotel room in London, poring over my presentation for an upcoming meeting with Real Edu UK. I knew that their use case was unique and would require a lot of custom configuration, so I wanted to make sure I had every detail covered. I had been working on the presentation for days, and wanted to make sure that I made a good impression on Emily Garethson, the CEO of Real Edu UK.

As I went through my presentation, I felt confident that I had covered all the necessary points. I had also prepared myself for any questions that Emily and her team might have. I took a deep breath and made my way to Real Edu UK's office.

As I walked into the meeting room, I was greeted by Emily and her team, including Amaka. I felt a rush of adrenaline as I started my presentation. Emily listened intently, nodding and asking questions as I went along. I could see that she was impressed with my knowledge and expertise.

As I went through the presentation, I noticed that Amaka was looking at me with admiration in her eyes. I felt a spark of attraction between us and couldn't help but smile. I made sure to answer her questions carefully and thoroughly, enjoying the opportunity to showcase myself.

By the end of the meeting, I felt a sense of accomplishment. Emily and her team had been impressed with my presentation, and I had gained their trust and respect.

As I stepped out of the elevator, I could feel the relief wash over me. The meeting with Emily Garethson and her team had been intense, but it had gone better than I expected. I smiled to himself, feeling proud of my work.

As I walked towards the exit, I heard Emily's voice calling out to me, "Mr. Williams, a moment of your time, please." I turned around and saw Emily walking towards him, accompanied by Amaka.

"Good job in there, Mr. Williams," Emily said with a smile. "I'm impressed by your expertise and the level of customization you've done. I'd like to discuss some scenarios that weren't captured in your presentation. Would you be available for dinner later tonight?"

I was taken aback. I wasn't expecting a dinner invitation from the CEO herself. "Yes, of course," I replied, trying to keep my excitement under control. "I would love to discuss the scenarios with you."

"Great," Emily said. "I'll send you the details. Have a good day."

I watched Emily and Amaka walk away, feeling a sense of accomplishment. I knew I had to put in more work to impress Emily, but I was up for the challenge.

***

Amaka sat at her desk in her office at Real Edu UK, her mind still buzzing from her meeting with me. She couldn't believe how impressed she was with me. She grabbed her phone and sent a text to Rebecca.

"Hey girl, just wanted to let you know how amazing Femi is. I was blown away by his brilliance and expertise. I think I might like him!" she typed.

Amaka hit send and leaned back in her chair, feeling a mix of excitement and nervousness. She couldn't shake the feeling that there was something special about Femi, something that drew her to him.

As she stared out the window, lost in thought, she couldn't help but blush as she read Rebecca's text message. She had tried to play it cool during brunch, but it seemed like her feelings for Femi were obvious to everyone, including Rebecca.

Amaka quickly typed out a response, trying to play it off. "What are you talking about? I was just impressed with his business acumen."

Rebecca's reply came back quickly. "Sure, Amaka. I know you better than that. You were practically swooning over him."

Amaka groaned and put her head in her hands. She couldn't believe she was being so obvious. But there was something about Femi that had her completely smitten.

Finally, she typed out a response to Rebecca. "Okay, fine. You caught me. I do like him. But don't tell anyone, okay?"

Rebecca's response was playful. "Don't worry, your secret is safe with me. But I have to admit, you and Femi would make a cute couple."

Amaka smiled to herself. Maybe there was something there with Femi. She was excited to see where things might go between them.

***

I arrived at the restaurant wearing a navy blue suit and a white shirt with a light blue tie. Emily wore a black dress that hugged her curves in all the right places. We exchanged pleasantries, and I could tell that Emily was excited to discuss the business proposal.

As we sat down, I pulled out my presentation and began to walk Emily through my plan. I answered all of her questions and could see the excitement growing in her eyes. However, as the night went on, I noticed Emily's behavior changing. She began to lean in closer to me, and her flirtatious tone increased.

I knew that he had to remain professional, but Emily's advances were making me uncomfortable. I tried to steer the conversation back to business, but Emily persisted, placing her hand on my thigh, leaned in and whispered in his ear, "You know, Femi, I can make sure you get everything you want. All you have to do is give me what I want."

My heart dropped as I realized that Emily was not only flirting with me but was also making her advances clear. I knew I couldn't risk jeopardizing the deal with Real Edu UK.

As the night went on, I couldn't help but feel uneasy about Emily's flirtatious behavior. I tried to steer the conversation back to business, but she kept veering off-topic. Finally, when Emily suggested we go back to her place for a nightcap, I knew he had to put a stop to it.

"I'm sorry, Emily, but I can't go back to your place tonight," I said firmly.

"Your place then," Emily pressed.

"Not tonight as well," I responded quickly.

Emily's expression changed from one of seduction to anger. "What's the matter, Femi? Don't you find me attractive?"

"It's not about that," I replied, my palms were sweaty. "I just don't think it's appropriate given the business deal we're working on."

Emily's eyes narrowed. "Is that so? Well, let me remind you, Femi, that I have the power to make or break this deal."

My heart sank again. I knew I had to tread carefully. Emily has a record of always getting what she wanted, she was going to be the next The Secretary of State for Education. "I understand that, Emily, but I assure you that my focus is on the deal and nothing else."

Emily's smile returned, but it was cold and calculating. "Well, the only thing I want you to focus on tonight is me. I 'll be in my car waiting for you, Femi. Five minutes, don't keep me waiting."

After some minutes, I stood up from the table, feeling my hands shake as I tried to grab my drink and downed it. I couldn't believe what was going on as I walked to the door by the valet, feeling a knot form in my stomach.

I saw Emily's Lamborghini parked by the curb, and she was sitting behind the wheel, waving at me to get in. I hesitated, but the look on Emily's face made me feel like I had no choice. I thought she was testing me.

I sat in the passenger seat of Emily's sleek green Lamborghini, she had her variety music playing as she drove by pretty fast within the city, we barely said anything to each other, my palms sweating as I watched the city lights blur by. I felt like I was in a dream, a nightmare, really. I had no idea what Emily wanted with me, when we had just met earlier in the day and now she was acting like she had met me before.

As we pulled up to a gated community, Emily punched in a code and the gates swung open. My heart raced as we drove up to a massive mansion. I had never seen anything like it in London.

"This is not Buckingham palace, right?" I asked.

Emily parked the car and got out, waiting for me to follow. I hesitated, but eventually stepped out of the car and walked up to her.

"Come inside, it is not," she said, leading me through the front door.

I followed her through the grand entrance hall, feeling small and insignificant. Emily led me to a sitting room, where she poured us both a drink.

"I'll get straight to the point," she said, handing me a glass. "I want you, Femi. I want you to be mine."

My heart sank again, normally, I would have had her anyway I wanted but I don't mix business with pleasure. "I'm sorry, Emily but you don't even know me," I said, setting down my glass. "I can't do that. I am here to do a job, and I can't let anything get in the way of that."

"You are here to do this," Emily made a gesture showing off herself. She paused a bit to take a sip of her drink. "I know you and you might not know, you used to be with someone close to me and she couldn't stop thinking and talking about you. It was always Femi, Femi this, Femi that, she showed me and the girls your picture. I know everything I need to know about you from her. What I didn't know was what I saw today when you showed up at the office today. You presented, answered all our questions, you did with such composure that you had me dripping wet," Emily said. She leaned in to me.

I sat on the couch, staring at this version of Emily, I was meeting for the first time. Emily grabbed my arm. "You can touch and have me everywhere, Femi. You're mine now."

"Who is she? Who is the girl you are talking about?" I asked as I started to give in to Emily's lustfulness and seduction.

"She was dickmatized by your big shaft, her name is Sophie," Emily kissed my neck.

When I heard Sophie, I tried to pull away, but Emily's grip was too strong. Her alter ego was ready to devour me, I realized I was in real trouble.

I had learned from my mistakes from messing with Sophie. I had to be smart with Emily, a lot was happening at the same time. I had one goal and that was to try to get the contract with Real Edu UK, Sophie might know where I am and might be able to find me.

I talked myself into sleeping with Emily, "Fuck it, let's go to your bedroom. I need a bigger space to put this big willy on you, because I don't know your body yet."

Emily relaxed on her grip, got up from me, stood up and helped me to my feet.

An excited Emily led me to her bedroom. She started kissing me at the door of her room. We made our way to her bed, our body entangled, passionately kissing and caressing each other's body. After our steamy sexual encounter, I got up to go to the bathroom. I had never felt so weak in my life. I stumbled out of bed and made my way to the bathroom, my head spinning and my vision blurring. I couldn't understand what was happening to him.

"I feel dizzy, did you put something in my drink?" I tried to reach for the bathroom door.

"No! Why will I do that?" A satisfied Emily who was still trying to catch her breath replied.

As I reached the bathroom, I felt my legs give out, and I collapsed to the floor. The last thing I heard before everything went black was the sound of Emily's panicked voice calling my name.

"Stop playing games Femi," Emily sits up, not sure if it was a prank.

When she realized I wasn't moving or responding, she got up from her bed.

I had fainted!

Chapter Nine

When I woke up, I was lying on a hospital bed. I groaned, feeling a sharp pain in my head, and tried to sit up, but a hand on my chest stopped me. I looked up and saw a nurse standing next to me.

"Take it easy, Mr. Williams," she said soothingly. "You had a bit of a scare last night."

My mind raced. I had no idea how I had ended up in the hospital, but I knew it couldn't be good. I tried to remember the events of the night before, but everything was hazy.

"What happened?" I asked, my voice hoarse, I could barely speak.

Emily and Amaka arrived at the hospital to visit me. As they approached my hospital room, Amaka couldn't help but wonder what had happened to me. Emily explained that I had suffered from food poisoning during our dinner the previous night.

As they walked into my room, the nurse was checking my vitals and documenting them on the chart. Amaka noticed that I looked pale and weak. The nurse looked up and noticed the two visitors. She introduced herself and informed them that I was doing better and would be discharged soon.

Amaka asked if everything was okay, and the nurse hesitated before revealing that they had found something strange in my blood from the tests they ran. She suspected that it might be the reason for my fainting episode. Emily and Amaka were shocked, and they both turned to me, I looked bewildered.

The nurse explained that they would need to monitor me closely to ensure that I didn't have an adverse reaction to medication. She also told them that they would need to conduct further tests to determine what they found in my system.

Amaka stood by my hospital bed, wringing her hands anxiously. She had never felt so guilty in her life. She reserved the restaurant that had given me food poisoning and thought it was entirely her fault. She took a deep breath and turned to Emily, who was standing beside her.

"I'm so sorry," Amaka said, her voice trembling. "I never should have chosen that restaurant. I didn't know it was going to make him sick."

Emily gave her a sympathetic look. "It's not your fault, Amaka. None of us could have known what was going to happen."

Amaka shook her head. "But I should have been more careful. I should have done my research."

I stirred in the bed, and Amaka rushed to my side. "Femi, are you okay?" she asked, her eyes filled with concern.

I looked up at her weakly. "I'll be okay," I said. "But you don't have to blame yourself, Amaka. It was just an unfortunate incident."

Amaka nodded, her eyes filling with tears. "I'm just glad you're okay, Femi."

I smiled weakly. "I'm tough, Amaka. I'll be up and about in no time."

Amaka gave me a small smile and turned to Emily. "What do we do now?" she asked.

Emily sighed. "We'll just have to wait and see how he recovers. He'll need some time to get back on his feet and hopefully he still wants to work with us because we really need the solution his company provides." She looked at Femi with a smile.

Femi responded with a fake smile, flashes of him in bed with Emily goes through his mind. He wondered if she had put something in the drink he had at her house.

After a few more minutes of conversation, the nurse came back into the room and provided the estimated time for Femi to be discharged and gave him some instructions on what to do when he got home.

***

Amaka closed the door of her office and picked up her phone to call Rebecca, her best friend.

"Hey, Rebecca," Amaka said, her voice shaking. "I think I might have poisoned Femi."

"What? What do you mean, Amaka?" Rebecca's voice rose in concern.

"I reserved the restaurant where Femi and Emily had dinner, and I'm afraid I might have ordered something that made him sick," Amaka said, tears welling up in her eyes.

"Okay, okay, calm down, Amaka. Did Femi say anything to you about feeling sick or anything like that?" Rebecca asked, trying to comfort her friend.

"No, but I heard from Emily that he was hospitalized with food poisoning after the dinner, and I went to the hospital to see him where he is being hospitalized," Amaka explained.

"Amaka, you need to take a deep breath and relax. You can't blame yourself for something that may not be your fault. We don't even know for sure that it was the food that made him sick. Maybe it was something else entirely," Rebecca suggested.

"I hope you're right. I'll keep you updated on any news," Amaka said, feeling a little bit better after talking to her friend.

"Why don't you go see him?" Rebecca asked.

"Are you sure? I don't even know where he stays in London," Amaka responded.

"Yes, I am sure. I will ask Biddy and will let you know, but you have to go see him, Amaka. And remember, everything will be fine," Rebecca reassured her before ending the call.

Amaka put her phone down and took a deep breath, trying to calm her nerves. She knew that she needed to focus on work, but her mind was still on Femi and the possibility that she might have caused his illness.

I was lying in the hospital bed, scrolling through my phone after responding to Tessa's text who has been asking for a meet up since our dinner, when I heard, "Hey, cuz! I heard you were in the hospital and I had to come see you," Bidemi exclaimed, dropping the bag of snacks he brought with him.

He stayed with me until the morning and we caught up on old times. My mood was lifted, and we laughed and joked around.

The next day, I was discharged from the hospital, and Bidemi offered to drove me back to the hotel.

As we drove, Bidemi couldn't help but tease me about my hospital gown.

"Man, you look like you're about to star in a hospital-themed movie," Bidemi jokes.

I laughed. "I know, right? But at least I'm out of that place now."

"Seriously though, what happened to you? Rebecca said you were poisoned or something," Bidemi asked.

I explained what had happened at the dinner with Emily and how I had fainted after having sex with her. I also told Bidemi about the narcotic-like materials found in my blood.

Bidemi shook his head in disbelief. "Man, you need to watch your back. You never know what people are putting in your food and drinks these days."

I nodded in agreement. "You're right. I need to be more careful. Tell Rebecca to let Amaka know that it wasn't her fault."

"What does Amaka have to do with this?" Bidemi asked, his eyes opened wider.

"Amaka made the reservation and meal options, Emily and I picked from," I responded wondering why Bidemi didn't know.

We arrived at the hotel, and Bidemi helped him with his bags. "Listen, man, I'm glad you're okay. If you need anything, don't hesitate to call me, okay?"

I smiled. "Thanks, Bidemi. I appreciate it. There is more to catch up on. London has been crazy and I haven't spent a month here."

Bidemi nodded. "Definitely. Take care, man."

We hugged, and Bidemi got back in his car and drove off. I was relieved to be back at my hotel and looked forward to getting back to work soon.

***

I sat up on the bed, my heart racing with anticipation as I read Tessa's message. I had sent her a message earlier to meet me at the hotel in the evening, but I didn't expect her to arrive so soon. I glanced at the clock on the bedside table and realized that I only had less than thirty minutes to get ready.

I quickly got up from the bed and started pacing around the room, trying to decide what to wear. I couldn't shake off the feeling of nervousness that was settling in my stomach. I wasn't so sure if I was fully recovered and knowing how the night might be because of what Tessa has been looking forward to doing since our last meeting at the restaurant. The last time I did the same activity Tessa is looking for us to do I fainted and now the night might end up being the same. Tessa didn't know I was hospitalized. She was expecting to see and spend time with the Femi she spent time with in Saint Tropez and the one she met in London for dinner with a lot of charisma, energy and good vibes, but now I wasn't sure if I was ready for it.

I stared at the mirror in my hotel room's bathroom, talking to myself, boosting my self confidence, "you got this, you are not going to be fazed or faint, you are the man." I said to myself, slapping myself, I made a strong face and sprinkled water on my face. I was still staring at myself when I heard a knock at the door.

My heart raced as I opened the door, expecting to see Tessa. Instead, I was met with Amaka standing there.

"Amaka, what are you doing here? How did you know where I was staying and my room number?" I asked, confused.

"Which one do you want me to answer first? Can I come in?" Amaka replied, trying to keep her voice down.

I hesitated but decided to let her in. I closed the door and turned to face her, waiting for an explanation.

"Rebecca told me where you stay here," Amaka said, smiling slightly.

I realize how the information trickled down from Bidemi to Rebecca and now to Amaka.

"I was worried about you and wanted to apologize for partially being responsible for you being poisoned." Amaka continued.

"Partially?" I cut in, raising my eyebrow.

"Yeah, cause you are partially responsible for eating the food. I am joking, I don't know what to say, I didn't know what to say to you but I guess this is how I deal with stuff like this. How can I make it up to you?" Amaka concluded. She looked uneasy and awkwardly acting in front of me.

I smiled slightly, my phone buzzed, I took a glimpse of the clock beside the bed and realized it was time to go see Tessa.

Amaka, still left in an awkward state, was expecting a response from me, who was trying to get my confidence back and gather my thoughts.

"You are heading to the Bahamas tomorrow with Rebecca right?" I asked.

"Barbados and yes," Amaka responded, wondering what he was trying to get at. She would have loved to stay here with him to make sure he was alright.

"Go to dinner with me on Wednesday when you come back," I said.

More confused, Amaka was speechless.

"And no, I am not trying to poison you. What's your phone number?" I bring out my phone and take Amaka's number.

I smiled. "Thanks for checking on me, I will see you Wednesday but I really need to rest."

"I understand," Amaka said, her face brightening up with a smile as she turned to leave. "Take care, Femi."

As soon as Amaka left, I let out a sigh of relief and checked my phone. It was a message from Tessa saying she was heading to the lobby. I quickly sprang into action, making sure everything was in order and that I looked presentable.

I had to think fast to avoid any awkward situation with Tessa, who was on her way to meet me. I quickly sent her a text message, telling her to meet me at the hotel bar instead of the room.

Meanwhile, Amaka made her way to the hotel lobby, feeling relieved that I was resting. As she walked past a woman in a stunning dress, she couldn't help but compliment her on her outfit. The woman smiled and thanked her, but Amaka didn't think much of it as she continued on her way.

Little did Amaka know that the woman in the stunning dress was Tessa, the very person I was meeting at the hotel bar. Tessa had arrived earlier than expected and decided to wear one of her best dresses to impress.

***

I walked into the hotel bar and immediately spotted Tessa sitting at a table near the window. I couldn't help but smile as I made my way over to her.

"Hi there," I said, leaning down to give her a kiss on the cheek.

"Hi," Tessa replied, grinning up at him. "I'm so glad we could finally meet up."

"Me too," I said, pulling out a chair and sitting down opposite her. "So, what would you like to drink?"

Tessa wanted a glass of red wine, and I signaled to the bartender to bring us a bottle. We chatted for a while, enjoying the warm ambiance of the bar and the gentle hum of conversation around us. When we finished our drinks, I suggested we move to the hotel restaurant for dinner.

Over dinner, we talked about everything from our favorite books to our career aspirations as children.

Our stories were similar but happened in different continents and now we are sharing it over dinner on the same table.

I found myself drawn to Tessa's easy smile and infectious laugh, and I couldn't help but feel a deep connection with her.

As we finished our meal, I took Tessa's hand and led her backup to my room. I opened the door for her and gestured for her to enter. The room was dimly lit, with soft music playing in the background.

"Wow, this is beautiful," Tessa said, taking in the luxurious surroundings.

"I'm glad you like it," I replied, moving closer to her.

We danced slowly, swaying to the music, our bodies pressed close together. As the song ended, I leaned in to kiss Tessa. It was a gentle, tentative kiss at first, but soon we were lost in a passionate embrace.

"I feel like I've known you forever," Tessa whispered, her eyes locked on mine.

"Me too," I replied, smiling softly. "I think I'm falling for you."

Tessa's heart swelled with happiness as she leaned in for another kiss. We spent the night wrapped in each other's arms, exploring each other's bodies, and falling more deeply in love with every passing moment. The thought of fainting had slipped my mind, we were both wine drunk, she pushed me to the bed, continued to slowly dance as she stripped, it was like she had practice a routine in her head or practiced it and she was brilliantly performing it, the bulge in my black fitted pants confirmed it, why is it so hot in this room, I can hear the air conditioner humming sound but I can feel a drop of sweat finding its way on my forehead, I removed my beige jacket, my eyes locked on hers and down to her bosom to her waist she continued to whine while slowly undressing herself. I unbuttoned my shirt so fast, I would have been gunning for the world record, that made her smile as removed her legs one after the other from her dress which is now on the floor. "I don't remember this beautiful body," I was mesmerized by her, she moved closer as soon as I tried to remove my pants. Tessa had me in ninth heaven before jumping on me to give me the ride of my life. She would grip my hip area tight every time she climaxed before falling on my chest while slowly bumping me. I turned her around and went pound for pound like the local currency and every time she let out a big moan, I whispered in her ear, "Is this what you came for? This is what you wanted, yeah?" She responded with her voice breaking, "hmmm hmmm", we continued passionately until I reached my climax as well, the skyline view of the city of London as our witness.

***

I spent the next few days with Tessa, exploring London, Oxford and Bath. I continued to gain my confidence as the days came. We had made our way to Bath and were staying at a cabin that belonged to Tessa's family.

The cabin in Bath, is a picturesque wooden structure surrounded by lush green trees. It has a charming front porch, a fireplace with two rocking chairs where Tessa and I had spent the previous evening, enjoying the cool breeze and sipping wine.

Inside the cabin, the cozy bedroom has a queen-sized bed adorned with fluffy white pillows and a soft duvet. Large windows allow natural light to stream in, providing a warm and inviting atmosphere. The walls are decorated with abstract paintings that add a touch of sophistication to the space.

As Tessa and I lay in bed in the morning, we could hear the gentle chirping of birds outside, creating a serene and tranquil ambiance. The room is decorated with flowers, adding a pop of color to the otherwise minimalistic decor. A wooden dresser and a closet provide ample space for their clothes and belongings.

The cabin's bathroom is modern and spacious, with a large bathtub and shower area. It has a natural, rustic theme, with wooden walls and a stone basin sink. Tessa had already taken a relaxing bubble bath earlier in the morning, and the sweet scent of lavender lingered in the air.

As we lay in bed, Tessa and I cuddled under the duvet, chatting and laughing, enjoying each other's company in the peaceful retreat. The cabin provided the perfect escape from our busy lives, allowing us to relax and rejuvenate in each other's company.

Tessa turned to me, I was lying beside her in bed, and took a deep breath before speaking. "Femi," she said softly, "I need to talk to you about something."

I turned to look at her, my eyes curious. "What is it?" I asked, sensing that this was an important conversation.

Tessa hesitated for a moment before speaking. "I know that you see other women," she began, her voice barely above a whisper. "And I want to be one of the women that you truly care for, not just a random one."

I looked at her, my expression serious. "Tessa, you're not just a random one," I said, I took her hand in mine. "I care about you deeply, I enjoy your company and I want to be with you. These past few days have been wonderful, and I have enjoyed every moment with you."

Tessa's eyes lit up, and she smiled. "Really?" she asked, feeling a sense of relief wash over her.

"Really," I confirmed, my thumb rubbing gently over the back of her hand. "I know that I've been seeing other women, but that doesn't mean that I don't have feelings for you. In fact, it's quite the opposite. I see a future with you, Tessa."

Tessa's heart swelled with happiness, and she leaned in to kiss me. "I see a future with you too, Femi," she whispered against his lips.

We stayed in bed for a while longer, enjoying each other's company and talking about our hopes and dreams for the future. For the first time, Tessa felt like she truly belonged with someone, and she knew that I was the one she wanted to spend the rest of her life with.

We parked our bags, got ready and headed back to London.

***

When we arrived at Tessa's luxurious apartment, I dropped her bags on the floor.

"Do you want water, sweetheart?" Tessa asked.

"Yes, please," I responded.
Tessa brought me water and stayed close to me hugged me not to leave as I dropped the glass cup I was holding.

" I will be back before you know it babe, I leave for Lagos right after the wedding. Let me know if you want to come to Lagos and if you can't, just know I will be back before you know it," I reassured her.

I kissed her forehead, raised her head and kissed her passionately. It quickly escalated, Tessa started unbuttoning my shirt, I stopped her knowing that I didn't want to spend the rest of my day there, which was going to happen if she was able to get me naked. I turned her, raised her dress up, slid her panties to the side and thrusted her, she gasped for air as she held on the couch. I continued to explore her body from behind. We both erupted with sexual satisfaction at the same time. Tessa loved it, she wanted and needed that till the next time she would see me. She knew I was busy but I was present when I was there and this for her was the gift she needed till the next time. She had fallen head over heels for me.

***

I walked into my hotel room with a sigh of relief, finally able to unwind after a long day of driving and excitement with Tessa. I dropped my bag by the door and headed straight for the bathroom, eager to wash off the day's stress.

After a hot shower, I dried off and checked my phone. I had several messages waiting for me, including ones from Maria, Catherine, Zeke, and Bidemi.

I sighed as I scrolled through them, knowing that I couldn't avoid them forever. I started to type out a response to each one, trying to keep my responses short and to the point.

As I worked my way through the messages, I couldn't help but feel a sense of unease. I had been seeing these women casually, but I knew that I needed to make a decision soon. I couldn't keep stringing them along forever. I would have married all of them if I was a king and lived in Nigeria but that isn't the case.

"Let me know when you are back in town, I dropped your tuxedo and *Agbada* attire with the receptionist, let me know if it fits," Bidemi's message read.

After finishing the messages, I set my phone down on the nightstand and leaned back against the pillows. I knew that I needed to focus on my upcoming meeting with Real Edu UK, but I couldn't seem to shake off the thoughts about my romantic life.

With a deep breath, I forced myself to push those thoughts aside and began to prepare for my final meeting with Real Edu UK. I had a lot riding on this one, and I couldn't afford to let my personal life distract me.

***

I walked out of Emily's office with a big grin on my face, feeling like I was on top of the world. I had just secured a five-year contract with Real Edu UK, and the thought of it made me incredibly happy.

As I walked down the hallway, I noticed Amaka standing at the end of it, waiting for me. She saw the expression on my face and knew that something good had happened.

"Hey, what's got you looking so happy?" Amaka asked, her eyes sparkling with curiosity.

I nodded, "Yeah, I am happy, I secured a five year contract with y'all instead of the two we were negotiating. It's a big win for my company."

Amaka walked closer to me and said, "Congratulations! That's amazing news."

I smiled, "Thank you! We will celebrate at dinner tonight. I'll pick you up at 8."

Amaka raised an eyebrow, "Pick me up? Where are we going?"

I chuckled, "It's a surprise. Just dress nicely and be ready by 8."

Amaka smiled, "I'll be ready. See you then!"

I walked towards the elevator feeling on top of the world. I couldn't wait to celebrate with Amaka tonight.

***

I drove to the coffee shop I was meeting Bidemi at.

"You've got this big grin on your face since you got here. Spill the bean bro," Bidemi inquired as he sat across the table from me.

I was still sipping his coffee with a smile on his face, and was taking my time.

"Did you smash her in her office after the contract? Talk to me bro, what happened?" An impatient Bidemi followed up with another question for me.

I put my cup down after sipping coffee. "I got a five-year contract with them, Biddy," I said, grinning.

"That's great news, man!" Bidemi exclaimed. "How did you do it?"

I leaned in, a mischievous glint in my eyes. "Well, I had to tease Emily a bit."

"Tease her?" Bidemi raised an eyebrow.

"Yeah, I knew she was hesitant about committing to such a long contract," I explained. "So I had to make her feel like she was missing out on something if she didn't sign with us." I gestured, pointing to myself.

"And it worked?" Bidemi asked.

I nodded. "It worked like a charm. I made her see the benefits of a long-term partnership, and she agreed to a five-year deal instead of the two years we initially negotiated. Plus, I subtly included that she owed me because I fainted in her house."

Bidemi chuckled. "You always know how to work your magic, Femi."

I grinned. "I just know how to read people and give them what they need."

"Who knew crazy Sophie was going to be useful to you, years after you ran away from her," Bidemi jokes.

"Thank you, Sophie!" I said.

We laughed!

I shared the announcement with my team in San Francisco, I sent a company wide email sharing the good news from London.

We soon left the coffee shop after some conversations about Bidemi's wedding rehearsal dinner and bachelor's eve party.

***

As I made my way towards the elevator at the hotel, I noticed a woman in her mid-forties standing by the elevator, trying to catch my attention. She was tall, with a fit and toned physique. Her blonde hair was styled in a sleek bob, framing her sharp cheekbones and piercing blue eyes. She wore a form-fitting black dress that hugged her curves in all the right places, and a pair of stilettos that accentuated her long legs.

"Excuse me," she said, flashing a smile in my direction. "Hi, I've seen you around here at the hotel and I wasn't sure I would have a chance to run into you again. I was wondering if you would like to join me for a drink."

I was amused by the sudden approach but managed to remain polite. "Thank you for the offer, but I'm afraid I have plans already," I replied, giving her a small smile before entering the elevator.

"My name is Charlotte, but you can call me Lottie," she stretched her hand towards me.

I looked at her, gave her a small smile and introduced myself. "What do you want, Lottie?" He asked.

A little shocked by how direct my response was, "I want to have drinks with you and have fun all night and you seem like a fun person or am I mistaken?" Lottie paused for a second.

"You are not wrong, and I do already have plans tonight. Maybe later?" I was going to continue to talk but the elevator indicated that it was my floor. "What's your room number? I will call you and set something up."

"I'm in PH 2," Lottie said as the elevator closed on both of them.

***

I was standing by the green Maserati I rented for my trip with Tessa, checking my phone for the time. I couldn't wait to see and spend time with Amaka. As I waited, I couldn't help but think about how beautiful she looked when we met earlier in the day.

When Amaka arrived, I was blown away by how stunning she looked in her black dress. As she approached the car, she hugged me, I opened the door for her, and she stepped in, admiring the luxurious interior.

As we drove to the restaurant, I couldn't take my eyes off of her. I felt so lucky to be spending the evening with her. The dinner was perfect, with candlelights and romantic music playing in the background.

After dinner, we decided to take a walk to a nearby rooftop bar. As we sipped on our drinks and looked out at the city skyline, I felt like I could talk to Amaka about anything. We shared our dreams and aspirations, and the conversation got more intense as the night wore on. Her dad was Igbo from Enugu, the eastern part of Nigeria, and her mom was Yoruba from Osun, the western part of Nigeria. Amaka was born in London, in the Croydon area and had a lot of

Nigerian influenced upbringing which helped shape her.

"Congratulations on your deal with Real Edu UK, I know Emily can be a hard one to crack and she does the best deal for the company and more wins for your company" Amaka raised her glass towards me.

"Thank you, I won more being here with you," I responded with a smile.

That got Amaka blushing and as we stood there, gazing at each other, I leaned in to kiss her. It was a soft and gentle kiss, but it soon turned passionate. Amaka had to stop me before things got too heated.

"Femi, I think I like you a lot, but we need to take things slow," Amaka said, looking up at me.

"I understand," I replied, looking back into her eyes. "I respect your wishes, be my wife and we can take things as slow as you want."

"Not the wife line," Amaka responded.

We laughed, hugged and continued talking for a while before I dropped Amaka off at her apartment. As I drove back to my hotel room, I couldn't stop thinking about Amaka and how much I wanted to be with her. There was something about her, she was soft, gentle and relaxed. It was like she trusted me with her life and somehow I knew I was up to the task. Like, I've been waiting for this opportunity my whole life.

***

I wasn't ready to call it a night yet so I made my way to the hotel bar, I noticed a woman sitting by herself, nursing a glass of red wine. As I got closer, I realized it was Lottie, the blonde British woman I had met earlier. I hesitated for a moment, wondering if I should approach her, but then decided to take a chance.

"Excuse me, is it okay if I join you?" I asked, flashing a smile.

Lottie smiled and gestured for me to take a seat next to her. "Of course, love. What can I get for you?" she asked, signaling the bartender.

"A whiskey neat, please," I replied, before turning back to Lottie. "So, what brings you here this evening?"

"Just needed to get out of my room for a bit," Lottie replied with a grin. "It can get a bit lonely up there all by myself."

We made small talk for a while, but soon the conversation turned to more personal matters. Lottie talked about her life in London, and I opened up about my work and travels.

After a few drinks and sending a message to Amaka, that I made it to the hotel and was calling it a night, I was feeling bold. "How do you like the penthouse in this hotel?"

Lottie smiled mischievously. "It is quite lovely, if I do say so myself."

"Would you show it to me?" I asked, feeling my heart rate increase.

Lottie finished her drink and stood up. "Follow me," she said, taking my hand.

We made our way to the elevator and rode up to the top floor. When we stepped out, Lottie led me down the hallway to her penthouse suite. As she opened the door, I was struck by a better stunning view of the city skyline.

As we entered, I was amazed by the luxurious interior. The large windows showcased a stunning view of the city skyline.

Lottie stepped up behind me and wrapped her arms around my waist. "I'm glad you like it," she murmured, pressing her lips to his neck.

The rest of the night was a blur of passion and desire. Lottie and I were lost in each other's arms, exploring every inch of each other's bodies. We both knew it was just a fleeting moment, but it felt so right in that moment.

As the sun began to rise, I gathered my things and headed back to my own hotel room, leaving Lottie asleep in her penthouse. Her boldness was the price she had to pay for an amazing night but I couldn't shake the feeling that I was the meat in the hot dog and she wanted a bite and I provided that, another satisfied woman, I should be given an award for keeping the peace.

Chapter Ten

"Love, Drama, and Fidelity: A Nigerian Wedding Tale."

It was a crisp Friday morning in London, the kind that makes you want to snuggle in bed a little longer. I had just left the penthouse, I spent the night with Lottie, again. I know what you are thinking, didn't he just mention that he had to make a decision and stop stringing all these girls along? I know I said that, it has been on my mind as well but there is just something about older women who are fit, sexy and know what they want plus I am not going to be in London forever, why not just enjoy it while I am here. The only I had to bring to Lottie is great conversations, energy and the big black mamba I am blessed with, she doesn't ask me for anything, we set an appointment and I show up with the best energy ready to have fun while fulfilling each other's fantasies, what more can I ask for after working hard the whole day, I spend my nights being well fed and pleasured and providing pleasure like the king that I am.

The sky was a soft shade of gray, and a light mist hung in the air, adding a mysterious charm to the city. From my high-rise hotel room, the view was spectacular. The Thames River flowed majestically, and the iconic Tower Bridge stood tall and proud in the distance. The city was alive, with red double-decker buses and black cabs buzzing along the streets, and the sound of chatter and laughter from the people below filling the air. In the distance, the Shard and the Gherkin towered above the skyline, reminding me that I was in one of the world's greatest cities. It was a peaceful and serene moment, one that made me feel grateful to be alive and in such a magnificent place.

I spent the day responding to emails and texts from Maria, Catherine, and Tessa, all expressing that they missed me. I was working on a proposal I was presenting to a company in Lagos in December when I got a text from Bidemi asking where I was. The wedding dinner rehearsal was about to start. I was Bidemi's best man. I had to quickly wrap up my work and drove to South Kensington in London, where the dinner rehearsal was happening.

As I entered the venue, I spotted Bidemi's mother, Mrs. Abiodun, a woman in her late 50s dressed in a traditional Nigerian attire, looking around for someone.

I approached her, "Good evening, Auntie. Is everything okay?"

Mrs. Abiodun turned around and smiled, "Oh, Femi! Thank goodness you're here. Bidemi has been looking for you everywhere."

I chuckled, "Well, I'm here now. What does he need?"

"He wants you to help him with his speech for tomorrow. You know how nervous he gets in front of a large crowd."

I nodded, "Sure, no problem. Do you know where he is?"

"He and Rebecca are in the back with the caterers, checking on the food. Come, I'll take you to him."

As we walked towards the back, I couldn't help but ask, "Auntie, may I ask what dish you recommend?"

Mrs. Abiodun grinned, "Oh, definitely the jollof rice. It's a family recipe, and everyone loves it."

I smiled and said, "I was going to try the pounded yam and egusi but now I have to go with the Jollof rice."

As we reached the back, Bidemi rushed over to them, "Femi, thank God you're here. I need your help with the speech."

I chuckled, "Yes, your mom already told me. Let's go over it."

We spent the next hour going over the speech, I offered suggestions and Bidemi took notes. After we finished, Mrs. Abiodun called them over for dinner.

As we sat down to eat, I couldn't help but think how lucky Bidemi was to have such a wonderful family. I glanced over at Mrs. Abiodun and said, "Auntie, this jollof rice is amazing."

Mrs. Abiodun beamed with pride, "I'm glad you like it, Femi. You know, you always have a home with us."

I smiled, feeling grateful for the kind words. "Thank you, Auntie. That means a lot to me."

Bidemi and Rebecca sat close to each other, holding hands and whispering sweet nothings to each other. Mrs. Abiodun, Bidemi's mother, sat regally at the head of the table, nodding in agreement with the wedding planner's checklist. Amaka and I were seated on either side of Mrs. Abiodun, making small talk, banter and low key flirting and enjoying the ambiance. Rebecca's parents sat beside Mrs. Abiodun and joined in the small talk.

The wedding planner, a tall and elegant woman with a clipboard, went through her checklist, ensuring that everyone knew what they were doing tomorrow. She looked up from her clipboard and made eye contact with Rebecca, who signed off on each item with a smile.

"Excellent," the wedding planner said, "That's everything. We'll have everything ready for tomorrow's ceremony."

Bidemi squeezed Rebecca's hand and whispered, "I can't wait to marry you tomorrow."

Rebecca smiled back at him and replied, "I can't wait to be your wife, Bidemi."

Mrs. Abiodun cleared her throat, drawing their attention. "It's going to be a beautiful ceremony tomorrow," she said, beaming with pride. "I'm so happy for both of you."

I raised my glass and spoke up, "Here's to Bidemi and Rebecca, may your love continue to grow stronger every day."

Everyone raised their glasses and toasted the couple. The atmosphere was filled with excitement and anticipation for the big day tomorrow.

"Let's go to your bachelor's eve party my guy," I said as I signaled Bidemi to get up.

Bidemi kissed his fiancee and said his goodbye to her and her family. As he approached the boys and I, there was a scream of excitement.

"Can you please watch him tonight, Amaka?" Rebecca asked.

"Are you sure you don't want me to be with you when you are performing your family traditions?" Amaka asked, feeling worried that she might not be supporting her friend at her family tradition.

"Do this for me, babe, that is all I need from you tonight, plus I see how you and Femi have been looking and flirting with each other" Rebecca said.

"You owe me one," Amaka responded.

They hugged and smiled.

***

The bachelor's eve party for Bidemi took place in a trendy London nightclub. As the best man, I had arranged the party, and spared no expense to make it an unforgettable night for Bidemi.

The club was dimly lit, and the music was loud. I had hired a DJ who played all of Bidemi's favorite songs, and there was a dance floor that was packed with people. Bidemi and his friends had a reserved table near the dance floor, and they were served with top-shelf drinks.

I invited a few dancers, and they entertained the party guests with their moves. Everyone was having a great time, and the atmosphere was electric. The club was filled with laughter and cheers.

Amaka showed up in a sleek hot pink dress that accentuated her curves, and she looked stunning. She had changed from the dinner attire she had on earlier. I was surprised to see Amaka walk in. She was dressed to the nines and looked stunning. I couldn't help but feel a flutter in my chest when I saw her. I had always found Amaka attractive, she is attracted to me as well, our dates and our continuous flirting at the dinner spoke volume, but I knew I couldn't act on those feelings, especially not tonight.

"Hey, Femi," Amaka said, giving me a warm hug. "I hope you don't mind me crashing the party. I just couldn't resist."

"Of course not," I replied, trying to keep my cool. "You're always welcome here."

As the night progressed, the party got more intense, and I had arranged for a surprise appearance by a famous Nigerian artist. The artist took the stage, and the crowd went wild. Bidemi and his friends danced and sang along to the artist's songs.

The party continued well into the early hours of the morning, and everyone was in high spirits. As we left the club, Bidemi thanked me for organizing such a fantastic night, and we all looked forward to the wedding day ahead.

Amaka and I made sure Bidemi made it to his hotel room in South Kensington.

"Babe, he is in his room now," Amaka sent a text to Rebecca.

As we walked towards the hotel lobby, I hesitated for a moment before asking, "Do you want to come up to my room for a drink? We can catch up some more."

Amaka's smile grew wider, and she nodded eagerly. We spent the rest of the night talking and laughing, enjoying each other's company. The conversation got intense and Amaka leaned in to kiss me. It started soft, I could feel her tender lips on mine but it got intense quickly. Amaka told me she loved how I carried myself at the party. She was excited and happy to be here with me and so was I. She loved how she felt around me.

"Are you sure?" I said, pulling her less than an inch away from my lips.
A speechless Amaka couldn't utter a word, she nodded and leaned back into me, it got intense and we spent the rest of night making love until the early hours of the morning. As we fell asleep in each other's arms, I knew I was in trouble, this type of trouble felt good but trouble regardless. I couldn't help but feel a strong connection with Amaka, I didn't care that she was Rebecca's bride-to-be's best friend and maid of honor. I didn't want her to leave.

***

I sat up in bed as I watched Amaka tiptoeing towards the door. "Where are you going?" I asked softly.

Amaka jumped at the sound of my voice and turned around to face me. "Oh, Femi," she whispered, "I didn't want to wake you up. I'm just going to help Rebecca get ready for the church wedding."

I nodded slowly, still trying to shake off the grogginess of sleep. "I see," I said. "You know you don't have to sneak out like a thief in the night, right?"

Amaka chuckled nervously. "I know," she said, "but I didn't want to disturb you. You looked like you needed your rest."

I smiled at her, my heart racing at the sight of her. "You know, you look beautiful in the morning light," I said, my voice low and husky.

Amaka blushed, feeling a sudden rush of heat to her cheeks. "Thank you," she whispered, "but I really have to go."

I nodded, feeling a dart of disappointment as I watched her slip out of the room. I knew I had to keep my feelings for Amaka in check, especially now that she was the maid of honor at Bidemi's wedding. But as I lay back down on the bed, my thoughts kept drifting back to her, flashes of last night at the top of my thoughts, here I was wondering if there was a chance for us at all.
I knew I needed to get up, get ready and make sure Bidemi was ready for his wedding.

***

The Grand Westminster Cathedral in London was the chosen location for Bidemi and Rebecca's church wedding. The cathedral was adorned with beautiful flowers and candles, with an orchestra playing soft music in the background.

I was dressed in a black tuxedo, and stood at the altar, beside Bidemi waiting for his bride-to-be to arrive. Amaka, looking stunning in her purple bridesmaid dress, stood on the side of the bridesmaids. As the organ music started, everyone stood up and turned to see the bride walking down the aisle on her father's arm.

Rebecca looked breathtakingly beautiful in her white wedding gown, with a long veil trailing behind her. As she reached the altar, her father gave her hand to Bidemi, who was dressed in a navy blue tuxedo. The couple exchanged their vows, promising to love and cherish each other for the rest of their lives.

After the ceremony, the couple, along with their wedding party, moved to a beautiful garden for their wedding photos. Guests congratulated the newlyweds, taking turns to take photos with the happy couple.

***

The wedding guests all went to the venue for the reception, which was less than three minutes from the church. The reception was held in a large banquet hall decorated with bright Nigerian colors and patterns.

As the DJ played the opening song for the wedding reception, I walked onto the dance floor with Amaka by my side. As Bidemi's best man and Rebecca's maid of honor, we were introduced and we dazzled the guests with our introduction dance as best man and maid of honor at Bidemi and Rebecca's lavish Nigerian wedding reception.

After the opening dance, Amaka and I stood with the other groomsmen and bridesmaid in front of the reception.

Bidemi and his bride, Rebecca, entered the reception hall to a thunderous applause and cheers from the guests. The DJ played their introduction song, and everyone stood up to welcome them. The couple danced into the hall with such grace and elegance, looking every inch the royalty that they were welcomed into the hall as husband and wife.

As Bidemi and Rebecca made their way to the center of the hall, guests started spraying them with money, in a tradition that was customary at Nigerian weddings. The sound of the money hitting the dance floor was deafening, and the couple laughed and danced to the beat of the music.

Amaka and I joined in the dancing, our eyes were focused on each other. We couldn't take our eyes off each other, and our chemistry was palpable. We danced closely, holding hands, and whispering sweet nothings to each other.

Amaka was wearing a stunning sequin lace dress that sparkled under the lights, while I was in my tailored *agbada*, looking dapper and handsome. We danced together, flirting and enjoying each other's company. Every time I went to get a drink, Amaka would go to the bar with me, and we would spend more time talking and laughing.

We were standing together, watching the other guests dance and enjoy the party. The music was loud, but we were close enough to hear each other speak.

Amaka joyous, "this has been such an amazing day. I can't believe my best friend is married now."

"Yeah, it's been quite the party. But I have to admit, I'm having more fun now that you're here," I responded.

Amaka smiles at me and takes my hand to slowly rub it.

"I feel the same way. It's been a long time since we've had a chance to hang out like this," Amaka said, still all smiles.

"I know. We should do it more often," I concurred.

"Definitely. Maybe we could go on a trip together sometime?" Amaka asked.

I nodded, looking into her eyes. "I would love that. Anywhere you want to go, I'm in."

Amaka laughs, swaying to the music.

"Well, let's not get ahead of ourselves. For now, let's just enjoy this moment together," Amaka said, still swaying to the music.

I pulled her closer and we continued dancing, enjoying each other's company as the party went on around us.

***

After the first round of dancing, Bidemi and Rebecca exited the dance floor to change into their traditional Nigerian attire. The guests took this opportunity to get drinks and mingle with each other.

A few minutes later, the MC announced the entrance of the newlyweds, and the crowd stood up and cheered as Bidemi and Rebecca made their way to the center of the dance floor.

Bidemi was dressed in a bright blue agbada with intricate gold embroidery, while Rebecca wore a

stunning green and gold *iro* and *buba*. The couple
looked stunning as they danced together, and the
guests cheered and clapped along to the music.

As they danced, Bidemi and Rebecca were showered
with more money, which they picked up and waved to
the crowd. The DJ played traditional Nigerian music,
and the couple showed off their dance moves, to the
delight of the guests.

As the wedding reception continued, I made a
touching speech, wishing the couple a lifetime of
happiness and love. Amaka, too, delivered a
heartwarming speech, celebrating her best friend's
love and marriage.

The wedding reception was filled with music, dance,
and laughter, with guests enjoying delicious food and
drinks.

I had been mingling with the wedding guests for a
while, making sure everyone was comfortable and
having a good time. I was chatting with some of our
family members when I felt a tap on my shoulder. I
turned around to see an older Nigerian lady in her
sixties, dressed in a traditional *iro* and *buba* outfit.

"Excuse me, young man," she said in a thick Yoruba
accent. "May I speak with you in private?"

I nodded and followed her to a quieter corner of the venue. "What can I do for you, ma'am?" I asked politely.

"My name is Jaiyeola," the woman said, clasping her hands in front of her. "I am a friend of the groom's family. I wanted to talk to you about something that has been on my mind since I saw you earlier."

I raised an eyebrow, curious about what this woman could want to talk to me about. "Sure, go ahead," I said.

Jaiyeola took a deep breath. "Young man, I have been watching you and I can see that you are a good person with a kind heart. I want to ask you for a favor."

I nodded, waiting for her to continue.

"I have a granddaughter," Jaiyeola said, her voice softening. "She is a good girl, but she is having a hard time finding a husband. I was wondering if you could help her, perhaps introduce her to some of your friends?"

I was taken aback by the request. I wasn't sure how to respond. "Uh, I'm not really sure how I can help, ma'am," I said carefully. "I don't know that many people here in London, and I don't want to make any promises that I can't keep."

Jaiyeola's face fell, and I felt a dart of guilt. "I'm sorry," I said quickly. "Maybe we can talk more about this later, when I have a better idea of how I can help."

"You don't seem to know who I am," Jaiyeola asked.

"I am sorry, I don't think we've met until now," I reassured her.

"I guess this UK weather has really done me some good then," Jaiyeola said with a smile on her face. "I am a big cousin to your dad, Jibby," Jaiyesola concluded, looking at me.

I realized only someone close to my parents knew my dad's nickname is Jibby. "That is awesome, how was he growing up?" I tried to redirect.

"He was a great kid to be around. Do you know why your parents are not here at your brother Bidemi's wedding?" Jaiyeola asked.

"I don't know, maybe they are busy with work or visa issues, the UK can delay response to some applications you know," I responded wondering why my parents didn't show up.

"Bidemi should have had a father figure here and it isn't like his father isn't alive, your brother should have had a chance to celebrate his wedding with both of his parents," Jaiyeola said as she adjusted her *iro* and *buba*.

"Wait. Excuse me, I don't think I completely understand you aunty. Do you mean Bidemi's father is alive and have not being in his life?" I asked. I was now curious and more vested in the conversation.

Jaiyeola smiled, "I won't say his father has not been in his life, he wasn't given the chance to be part of his life. He is in Lagos with his wife and they had visa issues from what you told me. Excuse me," she said as she walked away.

Chapter Eleven

I woke up with a start, sweat beads forming on his forehead and clothes drenched in sweat. He looked around, disoriented and confused, trying to get my bearings. Slowly, the memories of the night before came back to me. I had gone out for drinks with Tessa, and we had ended up back at her place. I had ended up with Tessa after the wedding, and never went back to my hotel.

I turned to my side and saw Tessa sleeping soundly beside me, her chest rising and falling in a peaceful rhythm. I couldn't help but admire her beauty, even in the dim light filtering through the curtains. Her hair was spread out on the pillow, framing her delicate features. I reached out to touch her face, but hesitated. I didn't want to wake her up.

Instead, I got out of bed and walked to the window, drawing the curtains aside. The early morning light flooded the room, revealing a cluttered but cozy space. Tessa had decorated her bedroom with colorful pillows, candles, and plants, giving it an artistic vibe. I could hear the distant sound of traffic from outside, but it was muffled by the double-pane windows.

I took a deep breath, trying to calm my racing thoughts. I realized that my nightmare was still haunting me. It has been a recurring dream for the past few days. In the dream, I was always running from something or someone, but I couldn't see what it was. I felt trapped and helpless, as if I was being chased by a ghost. I would wake up every time the ghost got close to catching up with me.

I shook my head, trying to dispel the negative thoughts. I didn't want to ruin my morning with Tessa by dwelling on my fears. I turned around and saw that she was awake, watching me with a curious expression.

"Hey," she said, stretching her arms. "What time is it?"

I checked his phone. "It's almost eight."

"Oh, wow," Tessa said, sitting up. "I must have slept in. I have to go to a work meeting today."

I nodded. "I should probably head out too."

Tessa got out of bed and walked to me, wrapping her arms around my waist. "You know you can stay here as long as you want right? Are you okay?"

I hesitated, then decided to confide in her. "I had the same nightmare again."

Tessa's face softened. "Do you want to talk about it?"

I shook my head. "Not really. I just need to clear my head."

Tessa nodded, understanding. "Well, you're welcome to stay for breakfast if you want. I am making your favorite"

I smiled, grateful for her kindness. "That sounds great."

***

"Do you want to grab dinner at this family owned Thai restaurant and talk?" Femi finally responded to Amaka's message.

"It's Thursday and he is just responding to my messages and numerous missed calls. Who does he think he is?" Amaka stared blankly at the city of London from her office while on the phone with Rebecca.

"I don't know what to tell you babe, I'd advise you to hear him out. He hasn't responded to Biddy's messages but he mentioned that he does that once in a while and that's normal for him to just up and leave," Rebecca responded.

"I don't know how to respond to his message, I don't know what to say," Amaka pacing back and forth in her office.

"Whatever you decide to do, I support. Tell him, sure, you'll meet him there. We just got to dinner."

"Bye babes," they both said, before cutting the call.

***

I sat nervously at a corner table in the bustling Thai restaurant, tapping my foot impatiently as I checked my phone for the time. I had been waiting for Amaka for almost half an hour, and I was starting to worry that she wouldn't show up.

I took a deep breath and looked around the restaurant, taking in the colorful decor and the delicious smells wafting from the kitchen. But my mind was elsewhere, wondering why Amaka hadn't called or texted to let me know she would be late.

Just as I was about to give up and leave, I saw Amaka's familiar figure entering the restaurant. I was relieved as she made her way towards me, her eyes lit up as she spotted me.

"Sorry I'm late," she said breathlessly, slipping into the seat opposite. "I got caught up at work."

I smiled, my worries melting away as I gazed into her warm brown eyes. "It's alright. I'm just glad you made it. I missed you," I said, looking at her with a smile.

"I missed you too, but you better have a good explanation on why I haven't heard from you till today and why you left the wedding without letting me know," Amaka adjusted her seat, staring directly into my eyes waiting for me to respond.

"Can I take your order?" The waiter said, looking at both of them.

I ordered a spicy papaya salad and a bowl of Tom Yum soup for her, knowing that Amaka always got the same thing no matter where we went.

She rolled her eyes, but I could see the smile playing at the corners of her lips. "Maybe I was planning to get something else this time." She said looking at me with a smile.

"Were you?" He asked.

"Nope!" She responded.

We both laughed.

I took a deep breath. "I've been thinking a lot about us lately, and I think we should give this a real shot. I know we've been flirting and spending time together, but I want to be with you, Amaka. I am always myself when I am with you. You get me?"

Amaka smiled, feeling a warm sensation in her chest. "Femi, I want that too. I just didn't know if you were ready for something serious. You still haven't told me why you went missing at the wedding."

"Excuse me, this is your food," the waiter said, putting their plates on the table.

We both dug into our food, savoring the flavors and enjoying each other's company. I couldn't help but steal glances at Amaka as we ate, feeling a mix of excitement and nervousness at being with her and what I was about to share with her.

I asked, "Can I trust you? I am about to share something that can make or break the trust between us with you. Can I trust you?"

I paused looking at Amaka who slowly nodded confirming that she can be trusted.

I explained everything that happened when I was pulled aside to talk to aunty Jaiyeola.

"You mean Bidemi might be your step-brother and not your cousin?" Amaka asked loudly, forgetting that they were in a restaurant. She contained herself, picked up her glass of water and drank from it.

I nodded and continued to provide more information regarding the situation.

"Does Bidemi know? What are you going to do?" Amaka reached out to hold my hand.

I took another deep breath. "I don't know what to do, Bidemi doesn't know." That wasn't what we were told when we were young. What I know about his father, was that he passed when he was young and that was the same thing he was told.

As we finished our meal, I paid the bill and we walked out of the restaurant together. The cool night air hit us as we stepped outside, and I felt a sudden urge to take Amaka's hand.

"Can I walk you home?" I asked, my heart beating fast in my chest.

Amaka smiled, taking my hand in hers. "I'd like that."

***

As we walked hand in hand to the train station, and we suddenly decided to go to a live show in outer London, we saw the ad on our way.

As we rode the train, Amaka rested her head on my shoulder, and I held her close. The train ride was short, and we soon arrived at the live show venue and settled in, enjoying the performance and each other's company. As the night progressed, we decided to head back to Amaka's apartment in outer London.

Once we got to Amaka's apartment, we sat on the couch sipping wine and continued our conversation. It was small but cozy, and we snuggled on the couch. I opened up to her about my fears and doubts, and she listened attentively, offering words of encouragement.

I took a sip of wine and looked at her, my eyes betraying the hesitation I was feeling. "I have to leave for Nigeria this weekend," I said quietly.

Amaka's expression shifted from one of enjoyment to one of concern. "Tomorrow? That's so sudden," she replied.

"I know. This morning, I got a call from my contact that the contract presentations started this week and my company's presentation is slated for next week. So I need to be in Lagos this weekend," I explained.

"I see," she said, her voice trailing off. "How long will you be gone?"

"I'm not sure yet. It could be a few weeks, I might just stay for *Detty* December before coming back to London in January."

Amaka took a deep breath and looked down at her glass, twirling it around in her hand. "Well, I hope everything goes well for you," she said softly.

I rubbed her hand, massaging it gently before kissing her cheek, "are you not coming to Lagos for *Detty* December?"

"I haven't thought about it till now," she replied, her voice barely above a whisper.
I hugged her from behind, my hands hovering her neck. She turned to face and lay on my chest.

***

I stirred awake the next morning, feeling the warmth of the sun on my face. I sat up and looked around, rubbing the sleep from my eyes. It took me a few moments to remember where I was: "Amaka's apartment," it finally clicked.

I smiled as memories of the previous night flooded back to me. We stayed up late, drinking wine and talking about everything and nothing. It was like time didn't exist and it was just us in the world. I felt content, almost happy, for the first time in a long while.

As I swung my legs out of the bed, I noticed a folded piece of paper on the bedside table. I picked it up and unfolded it. It was a note from Amaka.

"Good morning, handsome. I hope you slept well. I had to leave for work early, but I left you some breakfast in the kitchen. I wish you all the best in Lagos. Don't forget to call me when you get there. Remember, you're destined for greatness. Love, Amaka."

I couldn't help but smile at the kind gesture. I got up and followed the smell of coffee to the kitchen. There was a plate of toast and eggs waiting for me, along with a fresh cup of coffee.

As I ate, I thought about my upcoming trip to Lagos. I felt a mix of excitement and trepidation. I had not been to Nigeria in several years, and I was not sure what to expect. I knew that I would be meeting with some old friends, as well as some business contacts, but I was not sure how I would fit in.

After breakfast, I cleaned up the kitchen and got dressed. As I made my way to the door, I took one last look around the apartment, trying to consume every detail into my memory.

I stepped out into the bright London morning, feeling a sense of both excitement and apprehension. I knew I had a lot of work to do in Nigeria, but I was ready for the challenge. And I knew that, no matter what happened, Amaka would be there for me.

***

I returned to my hotel room in London feeling a mix of emotions. London has been more than what I had planned for, it has been a rollercoaster of emotions. I needed some time to sort out my thoughts and feelings.

As I settled in the room, I pulled out my laptop and dialed into a video call with Zeke and Cody. They gave me an update on our latest business dealings in San Francisco and discussed potential future projects. I listened intently, offering insights and ideas when necessary.

After the call, I checked his phone and saw messages
from Tessa, Maria and Catherine. I quickly replied to
all, catching up on their latest news and sharing my
own updates. I informed them that I might not return
till January and that I missed them.

***

I was filled with a mix of emotions as I touched down
at Murtala Muhammed International Airport in
Lagos. It had been years since I had last set foot on
Nigerian soil, and the sights, sounds, and smells of the
bustling airport brought back memories I thought I
had forgotten.

I was greeted at the arrival gate by an old friend, Wale,
who had promised to show me around the new
Lagos. Wale was a tall, lanky man with a bright smile
and an infectious laugh. We hugged each other like
long-lost brothers, and I couldn't help but feel
grateful for the warm welcome.

As we stepped outside the airport, I was struck by
how much Lagos had changed since I was last there.
The roads were wider, the buildings taller, and the
traffic more chaotic than I remembered. But despite
the chaos, I couldn't help but feel a sense of
excitement and anticipation.

Wale took me to a hotel in Victoria Island, I was impressed by the luxurious surroundings. The hotel was located in the heart of Lagos's financial district, and the view from my room was spectacular. I could see the glittering lights of the city and the shimmering waters of the Atlantic Ocean.

After settling in, Wale and I went out to explore the city. We drove through the crowded streets, passing by vendors selling everything from fresh fruits to second-hand clothes. The honking of car horns, the blaring of music, and the chatter of people filled the air.

I was amazed by the energy and vibrancy of the city. I had forgotten how much I loved Lagos, with its mix of cultures and traditions. As we drove past the famous Eko Bridge, I couldn't help but feel a sense of pride and belonging.

After a long day of exploring the city, Wale and I returned to the hotel exhausted but exhilarated. We headed to the hotel bar to have drinks. We settled at a corner, one of the servers came to ask us what drinks they'd like, we ordered drinks and began to catch up because it's been years since we've sat in person to talk.

The server brought our drinks, we cheered, glass clinked and both sipped the drinks.

"Wale is it me, or this girl is staring at me seductively,"
I asked, using my drink to point to the direction the
girl was seated.

"You are not wrong," Wale confirmed my suspicion.

"Did I miss something, Lagos girls used to be shy
back in the day," I expressed with surprise.

"That was then *o!* These new Lagos girls will *toast* you
while you are with your wife or girlfriend, they don't
care anymore," Wale informed me.

I shook my head before ignoring the girl winking and
constantly adjusting her bra and cleavage to show her
breast.

"Speaking of wives, I need to go back to mine, I am
sure she and the kids are missing me already," Wale
downed his drink, stood up and shook my hand with
a side manly hug.

"We go catch next week now, abi?" I asked.

"We go turn Lagos red for Friday, no worry," Wale assured.

As I lay in bed, listening to the sounds of the city
outside my window, I knew I was glad to be back to

Nigeria. I was excited to see what the future held in the vibrant and dynamic city of Lagos.

***

I woke up on a Sunday morning feeling refreshed and energized. As I opened my eyes, I was greeted by the stunning view of the Atlantic ocean from my hotel room. I couldn't believe how much Lagos had developed in the years I had been away. The skyline was dotted with high-rise buildings, and the streets were bustling with life.

I smiled to myself as I thought about the surprise I had planned for my parents. I had not told them I was coming to Nigeria, and I was excited to see the look on their faces when I showed up at their doorstep in Ikeja.

I got up from the bed and walked towards the window to take a closer look at the ocean view. The waves crashing against the shore created a soothing sound that helped me relax.

I had a quick breakfast, got dressed, and headed out to explore the city. I hired a cab for the day via the hotel desk and asked the driver to take me to the nearest market. The streets were crowded with people going about their business, and the air was filled with the aroma of street food. "This was a Sunday," he thought to myself.

After spending some time at the market, I headed to Ikeja to surprise my parents. As I got closer to their house, my heart started racing with excitement. When I arrived, I knocked on the door, and my mother answered.

"Surprise!" I exclaimed as my mother looked at me in shock.

"Femi, my son!" she cried out as she hugged me tightly.

My father came out of the living room, and he was equally surprised to see me.

"Welcome home, my son," my father said as he hugged me.

"You brought all these for us?" My mother asked, doing her celebrative dance going back and forth hugging me as the driver dropped off, the goodies we bought at the market and the ones I brought from London.

"*Oga that is everything.* Let me know if you need anything else, I will be in the car," The driver said.

"Thank you," I replied, closing the door.
"I am in the kitchen, I am making your favorite," my mom said as I made my way back into the house.

"Pounded yam and egusi soup?" I asked, joyous as a kid.

"Yes, the real, Pounded yam and egusi. I am making it myself, the way you like it," my mom responded.

"You've not been here for thirty minutes and you've already put my wife to work," my dad said jokingly.

"I'm sorry, dad. I know you also enjoy the egusi soup, the way she makes it," I said as I sat not too far from him.

"One of the many reasons I married my Peju. My Olapeju, *Olapeju mi*," my dad said, staring at the TV.

"Chelsea plays Newcastle today, I almost missed it. I thought you weren't a Chelsea fan," I asked looking at my dad who didn't give me a peep but was fully focused on the TV.

"I am Chelsea fan, it would be boring and sad if we all supported the same team and they lost, so I supported anything Chelsea was playing against. A win-win situation if you ask me," my dad responded, still glued to the TV.

"That makes sense, Ronke and I have always thought you didn't like Chelsea or the team we supported," I replied.

"Well, now you know. Can you grab me a beer in the fridge?" my dad asked.

"I haven't been here for an hour and you've turned me into an errand boy," I responded.

My dad looked at me and we both laughed.

"That was a good one. Where is my beer?" my dad asked.

Moments later, I arrived with the beer, my dad had his hand stretched. "I can see you, give me my beer."

He drank his beer directly from the can. "The beer of the elders is the right one for the harmattan weather."

We both laughed.

My dad readjusted himself on the couch and said, "so tell me, how's work? How's your company?"

"Dad, that is why I'm back in Lagos early," I said, looking up at him.

"Your company?" my dad raised an eyebrow in surprise. "What do you mean?"

I took a deep breath before launching into an explanation of the recent developments with my business, including my partners Zeke and Cody, and our plans to expand into Nigeria, now that we have two contracts signed in the UK.

"I believe there are a lot of opportunities for our business here in Nigeria, and I wanted to come back and explore those opportunities," I said, hoping my dad would understand.

my father nodded thoughtfully, taking in the information. "I see," he said finally. "And what are your plans now that you're here?"

"I plan to meet with some potential partners and contacts, as well as explore the market and see what is currently offered here in Nigeria. I have a presentation on Thursday with XG Ventures, remember Wale? He is my current contact and has been keeping track of XG for us and they moved their presentations to this past week and this week," I explained.

My dad nodded again, looking impressed. "Well, it sounds like you have a solid plan," he said. "I wish you all the best with your business endeavors here in Nigeria."

I breathed a sigh of relief, feeling grateful that my father was supportive of my plans.

Momentarily, we both screamed, "Goal!", with both of them having a fist pump in the air, Chelsea football club had scored.

"Like father, like son," my mom said as she walked towards us to let them know food was ready, advising them to eat during halftime so the food doesn't go cold.

Soon enough, it was halftime. My dad and I, high-fived a wonderful performance by the Chelsea team as we both stood up and headed to the dining table.

I sat at the dining table with my parents, relishing the aroma of the pounded yam and egusi soup my mother had prepared. I took in a deep breath and closed my eyes as I savored the smells wafting up from the steaming hot food.

"Ah, mommy, this smells divine," I said as I opened my eyes and looked at my mother, who was beaming with pride.

"I'm glad you like it, my son," she replied, handing me a bowl of the pounded yam and a spoon to go with it.

"No spoon needed mom, I am using my hand," I returned the spoon to the rest of the set and washed my hands.

I dipped my hand into the bowl of pounded yam, followed by the soup and scooped up a generous amount, putting it to my mouth. I closed my eyes and let out a sigh of satisfaction as the flavors of the soup and pounded yam blended together in his mouth.

"Mom, you still make the best pounded yam and egusi soup," I said as I took another mouthful.

"Thank you, my son. I'm glad you still remember your roots," my mother replied with a smile.

My father sat across from me, nodding in agreement. "Your mother is the best cook in the whole of Nigeria," he said proudly.

"Darling, not the whole world?" My mom asked her husband.

"I can confirm Nigeria but the whole world, I will be lying to you now," my dad replied.

"Lie to me, I don't mind, lie to me," she responded.

"I will start lying to you tomorrow, but not today," my dad puts another combination of pounded yam and egusi in his mouth.

I smiled as I continued to eat, enjoying the taste of the food and the warmth of being with my family. It was good to be back home and seeing my parents sharing the love they did.

"UB! Can you take these plates to the kitchen?" My mom called out the house help to come clear the table.

"Thank you, UB," my mom said, bringing out her phone to show me a picture of me at Bidemi's wedding.

"Look at you looking dapper in this picture, that was posted in the family group chat on Bidemi's wedding. How was the wedding?"

"The wedding was awesome, it was great to see Bidemi marry his wife. They looked awesome together," I said.

"That is good to hear you say about your brother," my mom said.

"Is he my brother?" I asked, looking at my parents.

"What do you mean, if he is your brother? He is your brother, I've always called him your brother," my mom responded quickly.

I took a deep breath, "I'm sorry mom, let me be precise with my question. Is Bidemi dad's son? I found out recently that he's my stepbrother," I said, watching their reactions carefully.

There was a moment of silence as my parents absorbed the news. Finally, my mom spoke up.

"How did you find out?" she asked.

"It doesn't matter how I found out," I replied. "The point is, I never knew, and I think it's important that we talk about it.

My parents are feeling a mix of emotions.

My dad nodded slowly. "I know it's not something we've talked about before, but it's true. After Bidemi's father died, I was there for his mother, and one thing led to another."

I took a deep breath, trying to process the news. "I can't believe you never told me," he said, feeling a sense of betrayal.

My mom jumps in, "It's not easy to tell you that, and it wasn't something that was easy to deal with for me as well. Your father might have his reasons for not telling you and I appreciate him for that.

My dad reached out to hold his wife's hand.

My mom sobbed and continued, "your dad had to do what he did due to tradition. When Bidemi's father passed away because of cancer, it was customary for him to take on the responsibility of his brother, Jide's wife and children if he had children. In this case Jide didn't have kids with Efosa, Bidemi's mother. Your dad spoke to me about it, I knew of our tradition as Yoruba people, especially within his family, we both agreed to bring her in to live with and gradually integrate her into our family. Efosa didn't want to move in with us, she wanted to stay at her husband's house. We were all devastated with Jide's death. Your father agreed to take care of the bills in both houses and check-in with her, spending one or two nights there. I soon got pregnant with you and months after that, your father told me that Efosa was pregnant as well."

My mom paused to clean tears from her face.

"I am sorry mom, I didn't mean to open up old wounds," I said feeling bad about the question he asked.

"It's fine, you need to know for the future of this family and for you and your sister's stake. Efosa soon gave birth to Bidemi and after a year, moved to London, she told the whole family that she had given them what they needed from her union with the Williams family. Your dad tried to persuade her to stay but she left for the UK without letting anyone know, she later married some guy, hence the Abiodun last name she now uses. Your father and I decided to move on with our lives after the whole drama but somehow you and Bidemi kept in touch and became close. I knew this day would come but we didn't know when. We didn't want it to change how you saw Bidemi," my mom said, reaching across the table to take my hand. "He's still your brother, no matter what."

There was another moment of silence as we all sat with our thoughts. Finally, my dad spoke up.

"We didn't tell you because we wanted you to have a normal relationship with Bidemi. We didn't want his mother wanting a different life, to define your relationship with him."

I nodded slowly, understanding where my father was coming from. "I get that, but it still hurts that you kept it from me."

"I'm sorry, son," my dad said, looking remorseful. "We should have told you sooner."

I sighed, feeling conflicted. "I guess he is my stepbrother," I said, adjusting myself on the dining chair. "I guess you have to figure out how to tell, Ronke?"

My parents looked at eachother, speechless.

Chapter Twelve

"The Detty December Ghost."

I had been staying in Lagos for a few days now, and each day was packed with activities. I woke up to the familiar sounds of cars honking and people shouting on the streets of Lagos. I got dressed in a traditional Nigerian outfit, a *buba* and *sokoto*, and made my way to the seating area of the hotel room where I met Wale, a colleague, and business partner.

We spent the morning going over the presentation for a potential client in Lagos, making sure everything was perfect. We discussed strategy, pricing, and possible objections the client may have.

After hours of preparation, Wale and I went to have lunch at one of the popular restaurants in Lagos. We had jollof rice and grilled fish, and I enjoyed every bit of the delicious meal.

Later in the evening, I met up with some old friends at a bar in Victoria Island. We shared stories of our time in school, talked about our careers, and laughed at old jokes. I enjoyed being around people who knew me before I left Nigeria, and it reminded me of the good times I had before I left.

As I walked back to my hotel room, I thought about the conversation I had with my parents about Bidemi. It had been a tough conversation, but one that had brought some clarity to our family dynamics. I was grateful to have the support of my parents, even as I navigated the complexities of my family's past.

My thoughts were interrupted by the sound of my phone ringing. It was Amaka. We caught up on the phone, Amaka filled me in on the latest gossip from London and I told her about my business trip to Lagos so far.

After our conversation, I returned to the hotel room and spent some time going over my notes for the presentation. I was feeling confident about our chances and was excited about the presentation tomorrow.

***

I woke up early the next morning and headed straight to XG Ventures' office, located in the bustling city center of Lagos. The presentation was scheduled for 11 am, and I wanted to make sure I had enough time to prepare and rehearse.

Upon arrival, I was greeted by a friendly receptionist who directed me to the conference room where the presentation would take place. As I waited for the XG Ventures team to arrive, I went through my notes one final time, making sure I had all my facts and figures in order.

At precisely 11 am, the XG Ventures team walked in, led by the CEO, Mr. Adekunle. I stood up to greet them, feeling a bit nervous but confident in my pitch. As I began my presentation, I could feel the room warming up to my ideas. The XG Ventures team seemed impressed with my thorough research and the detailed business plan I had put together.

As the presentation drew to a close, I could sense that I had made a good impression. Mr. Adekunle congratulated me on a job well done and promised to get back to me in a few days with their decision.

Relieved and excited, I left the XG Ventures office feeling like I had accomplished something great. I didn't like to celebrate before confirmation from the other party even though I knew I knocked the presentation out of the park.

"I don't have any doubt, you did great in there," Wale said reassuring me as we walked to his car. "I am hungry, let go to this restaurant I know you'll like," Wale concluded as we both got in his car.

***

Wale took me to one of Lagos' famous seaside restaurants. Over a delicious meal of fresh seafood and cold beer, we caught up with some of our old friends, reminiscing about old times and discussing our plans for the future and why I was in Nigeria.

While still at the restaurant, later that day, I received a call from Mr. Adekunle, who informed me that XG Ventures had decided to invest in my company and all their companies will utilize the services my company provides and lastly, that I needed to talk to Wale before they send the contract for me to sign.

Overjoyed, I couldn't wait to share the news with Wale. Wale soon received a phone call and didn't say much other than. "Yes sir. I understand sir. Thank you, sir. I will let him know, sir."

Wale looked nervous as he relayed the message to me, "XG Ventures is demanding a kickback of ten percent on all your business in Nigeria. They want to be compensated for the business connections they will provide to you."

I was surprised and upset. "What? Ten percent? That's outrageous! We didn't discuss anything about a kickback when we talked about the contract details."

"I know, Femi. But they are insisting on it, and we don't want to jeopardize the deal. I think we need to negotiate with them and find a way to minimize the impact on our business," Wale replied.

I rubbed my forehead, deep in thought. I knew that XG Ventures had the power to make or break our business in Nigeria. But I couldn't imagine losing such a huge percentage of my profits to a third party. "Let's see what we can do. I'll speak with Zeke and Cody and see if we can come up with a compromise that works for everyone."

Wale nodded in agreement. "I'll set up a meeting with the XG Ventures team, and we can try to work something out. But we need to be careful. This is a delicate situation."

I knew Wale was right. I couldn't afford to make a misstep in my new venture in Nigeria. I made a mental note to be cautious and strategic in my next move.

We went back into the restaurant to join our friends to continue catching up and making jokes of old times.

“Guys, I have to take Femi back to his hotel to change, we will catch up with you all later, tonight?” Wale said he tapped my shoulder for us to leave.

As we got into his car, Wale leaned back in his chair, a wide grin spreading across his face. "We did it, man. The deal with XG Ventures is done. This calls for a celebration. We're hitting the club tonight!"

I leaned forward, a serious expression on his face. "Wait, what did you say about XG Ventures?"

"We just closed the deal with them. They want ten percent of all our business in Nigeria," Wale said, still grinning.

My face fell. "Ten percent? That's a huge chunk of our profits. I'm not sure I'm comfortable with that."

Wale waved his hand dismissively. "Come on, man. We need this deal. It's worth it. Besides, we can negotiate the terms later. Right now, we need to celebrate."

I hesitated, still uneasy about the deal. "I don't know, Wale. I think we should think this through."

But Wale tapped me on the shoulder. "Don't worry about it, man. Let's just have some fun tonight. My wife knows I'm not coming home, so we can party all night."

I sighed, realizing I wasn't going to change Wale's mind. "Okay, let's go celebrate. But we need to talk about this more tomorrow."

***

Wale and I stepped out of the hotel, looking sharp. I wore a crisp white linen shirt, dark blue trousers, and brown leather loafers. I finished the look with a gold wristwatch and a matching gold chain around my neck. Wale, on the other hand, opted for a more casual look with a black T-shirt, ripped jeans, and a pair of sneakers. He accessorized with a silver chain around his neck and a black leather bracelet on his wrist. The streets of Victoria Island were bustling with activity as they made their way to the bar.

We decided to stop at a bar to start the night off. Inside, we ordered drinks and stood by the bar chatting and laughing. As we sipped our drinks, Wale and I caught the attention of some girls who were also hanging out at the bar. I was intrigued by one of the girls, a tall and elegant lady with long black hair. She had a sweet smile that lit up her face. I walked up to her to introduce himself, Wale followed suit.

"Hi there, I'm Femi," I said, extending his hand.

"Hi Femi, I'm Kemi," she replied, taking my hand and shaking it.

I couldn't help but admire Kemi's beauty. "Nice to meet you, Kemi. I must confess, you are the most beautiful thing I've seen since I got to Lagos."

Kemi smiled, flattered by my compliment. "Thank you, Femi! What brings you to Lagos?"

"Well, I'm here for business, but I'm also here to reconnect with my roots. My parents are from Lagos, and I was born in Lagos but I haven't been home as an adult," I explained.

Kemi nodded in understanding. "Wow, interesting. You sound like a busy man."

I chuckled. "Yes, I am, but I always make time for the finer things in life, like meeting beautiful women like yourself."

Kemi laughed, charmed by my smooth talking. "You're quite the smooth talker, Femi. But I like it."

I grinned. "I'm glad to hear that. And what brings a gorgeous woman like you to this bar tonight?"

"Just looking to have some fun and meet interesting people," Kemi replied.

I leaned in closer. "I've been trying to learn more about my culture lately. Maybe you can show me around?"

Kemi's eyes sparkled. "I'd love to. I know all the best spots in Lagos."

I couldn't help but admire Kemi's black dress. "By the way, I haven't been able to keep my eyes off of that black dress on you."

Kemi blushed. "Thank you, Femi. You look pretty sharp yourself."

I grinned. "I try my best. But I have to admit, you make it hard for the beautiful women in Lagos to compete."

Kemi chuckled. "Flattery will get you everywhere, Femi. I can tell you are trouble."

I raised an eyebrow. "Oh, am I now? Maybe you're the one who is trouble."

Kemi playfully rolled her eyes. "I don't know about that. But I can tell you're a charmer."

I grinned. "You're not so bad yourself. Maybe we should get out of here and go somewhere more private."

Kemi smiled seductively. "I like the way you think, Femi. Let's go."

I turned to Wale, grinning as I spoke. "I'll meet you guys at the club. Kemi and I are going to grab something from the store down the street."

Wale smirked, giving me a knowing look. "I see what's going on here. You're not fooling me, man."

I laughed, shaking my head. "You got me. I'll catch up with you later."

Kemi linked her arm with mine, a playful smile on her lips. "Don't worry, I'll make sure he gets to the club safely."

I smiled back at her, enjoying the warmth of her touch. "I have no doubt about that." I turned to the other girls. "Kemi and I will meet you guys at the club. We want to get some stuff at the store down the street."

The girls nodded, their eyes trailing after Kemi and I as we made our way out of the bar.

As we got out of the bar, the pulsing energy of Lagos on a Friday night surrounded us. Kemi leaned in closer to me, her voice low and sultry.

"I can't wait to show you around Lagos," she whispered.

I grinned, feeling a sense of excitement and anticipation building inside me. I was looking forward to spending more time with Kemi, learning about the city and discovering all of its hidden gems.

As we walked down the street, Kemi reached for my hand, entwining her fingers with mine. She looked up at me, her eyes shining with an intensity that took my breath away.

"I'm glad I met you tonight, Femi," she said softly.

I felt my heart skip a beat, player mode activated. I knew my charm was making this beautiful woman get the hots for me, and I was looking forward to the rest of the night.

"Me too, Kemi," I replied, squeezing her hand gently. "Me too."

Kemi and I made our way to my hotel room, our hands still locked. As soon as the door clicked shut, I turned to face her and drew her in for a kiss. Kemi eagerly responded, and our lips met in a passionate embrace.

As we broke away from the kiss, I couldn't help but admire Kemi's beauty and sexiness. Her long braided hair cascaded down her back, and her eyes sparkled with desire.

"Wow," Kemi whispered, her eyes taking in the view from the window. "This is incredible. Lagos looks beautiful from your room."

I grinned, pulling her towards me once more. "Not as incredible as you," I murmured, my lips brushing against her neck.

Kemi shivered with pleasure as I continued to kiss and nuzzle her neck. She reached up to run her fingers through my hair, her body responding to my touch.

I moved my hands down her body, my fingers tracing the curves of her hips. Kemi moaned softly as my touch ignited a fire within her. I walked her to the tall windows, our lips still passionately locked, her back against the window. We continue to explore each other's body. I moved the strap of her dress and bra to kiss and caress her voluptuous bosom, I felt her and she had no panties on, I raised her dress up before passionately bending her over thrusting her.

As we explored each other's bodies, Kemi and I found our way to the bed, still lost in the moment.

The sounds of our passion filled the room, and time seemed to stand still.

Finally, as we lay tangled together, our breathing ragged and hearts racing, I pulled Kemi close and whispered in her ear, "You're amazing."

Kemi smiled contentedly, still lost for words, felt a warmth spread through her body. She knew that this was just the beginning of an unforgettable night with Femi.

"Ready to head to the club?" I asked, a mischievous glint in his eyes.

Kemi laughed, "my legs are still shaking Femi."

I smiled, that sounded like music to his ears. "Are you okay?" I asked.

"Absolutely, Femi. I can't wait to see what kind of trouble we can get into," Kemi said, she looked at him with satisfaction and fulfillment but wanted more.

***

Kemi and I arrived at the club to find Wale and our friends waiting for us at the VIP session. The room was dimly lit, and the DJ's music filled the air. I felt

Kemi's hand in mine, and I led her towards our friends.

The group welcomed us, and we started dancing immediately. The night was young, and the drinks were flowing freely. The bass of the music was so strong that I felt it vibrating in my chest. I felt alive, and the energy of the club was contagious.

Kemi danced close to me, and I couldn't resist pulling her in for a kiss. She tasted sweet, and her lips were soft against mine. We explored each other's bodies on the dancefloor, with Kemi teaching me all the new dance moves.

As the night went on, Kemi introduced me to another girl she had brought with her. I felt the thrill of the night intensify as I found myself between two beautiful women. The three of us danced together, and the chemistry between us was touchable.

Eventually, Kemi and the other girl whose name I didn't get because of the loud music in the club danced with each other for a bit, they took a sneak look at me from time to time while I was chatting with Wale, who seem to be having a good night but a little jealous with the type of night I was having, "you are a married man," I said jokingly. "*Forget that thing,* this is Lagos, one day I will be lucky like you," Wale responded. I shook my head at Wale's response, I just finished pouring myself a drink when Kemi came back, leaned into me, her left hand rubbed my crotch and whispered in my ear that it was time to go back to the hotel room. We spent the night exploring each other's bodies, lost in the pleasure of the moment. I didn't know if it was just a one-night thing, but I couldn't help but feel grateful for the experience as Kemi and Ada switched positions on me. Kemi was still a bit satisfied from earlier as she allowed Ada jump on the driver seat, she rode me like her life depended on it as she held the joystick with her vagina walls, while Kemi got me distracted with her soft lips on mine, kissing on my neck, nipples and letting me play and caress her bosom. After Ada and I both climaxed, she tagged Kemi in who cleaned me up with the hotel towel before sucking on the black berry, in no time she woke up the black mamba. I had Kemi in the doggy position and Ada waiting her turn as she watched her friend moaning in pleasure, she couldn't wait so I had them both in that position thrusting like a horse in heat. Kemi climaxed in no time, her legs evidently shaking, I had to put Ada in a more submissive position for her to climax. What a night it was as I ended up like a black berry lollipop in her mouth.

As the sun began to rise, I lay in bed, exhausted but content.

"Bye, Zaddy," The girls said as they closed the door behind them.

I knew that I would always remember this night, and the memories would stay with me forever.

***

Wale and I met up for breakfast to catch up on the events of the previous night. We sat down at a hotel café, with the sun beating down on our faces, while the sound of the city filled our ears.

"So, how was the rest of your night, man?" Wale asked, taking a sip of his coffee.

I grinned, my eyes lighting up with a mischievous glint. "Let's just say, it was eventful."

Wale raised an eyebrow, a smirk forming on his lips. "Oh, do tell."

I recounted the events of the previous night, the club, the dancing, and the two women I had spent the night with. Wale listened intently, nodding his head at all the right moments.

"Sounds like you had a good time, man," Wale said, grinning. "I'm glad you're enjoying Lagos."

I chuckled. "Yeah, it's been great so far. I didn't know Lagos was this wild man. How was your night?"

Wale's grin widened. "Oh, you know me, always a good time. But I think I need to slow down a bit. My wife wasn't too happy with me staying out all night."

I chuckled. "I can imagine. Didn't you say, she knew you weren't spending the night at home? But hey, you only live once, right?"

Wale nodded in agreement. "That's true. Anyway, let's grab some food. I'm starving."

I nodded, and we ordered breakfast.

Wale took a sip of coffee before breaking the silence. "Hey, Femi, do you remember a girl named Moji?"

I furrowed my brow, my mind sifting through old memories. "Moji? Yeah, I remember her. We used to be best friends before I left Nigeria."

Wale nodded, a hint of mischief in his eyes. "Well, I gave her your number last night. She kept asking for it after she saw you on my social media."

My eyes widened in surprise. "You did what? Wale, come on, man. I don't want any drama."

Wale chuckled, leaning back in his chair. "Relax, Femi. She just wants to catch up with you. And who knows, maybe you'll hit it off again."

"Hit it off with a married woman? I don't want *wahala*!" I sighed, my mind racing. I hadn't spoken to Moji in years, not since I left Nigeria to pursue my dreams in the United States. Part of me wanted to reconnect, to see how she was doing and reminisce about old times. But another part of me was afraid of what I might find, afraid that the years and distance between us had created an unbridgeable gap.

Wale grinned, raising his coffee cup in a mock toast. "My friend, you never know what might happen. Life is full of surprises."

Our food arrived, we ate, talked about business, sports, life, and everything in between.

My phone buzzed, and I glanced at the screen to see a message from Moji. My heart skipped a beat as I read the text, asking if we could meet up. Wale's words echoed in my mind - life is full of surprises.

I turned to Wale, a mix of excitement and nervousness in my voice. "Wale, Moji just texted me. She wants to meet up."

Wale grinned. "Well, well, well. Looks like we might be in for another surprise, my friend."

I couldn't help but feel a mix of emotions as I thought about seeing Moji again. We had been best friends, and part time lovers growing up in Lagos, but I left the country to further my education in the United States, without telling her because I could tell she wanted more from me but she was also dating Kunle and I couldn't be an option for her.

As we finished breakfast, I couldn't help but think about what the day might bring. I waited a bit before I typed a reply, telling her I would be happy to meet up.

I couldn't help but feel nervous as I waited for Moji's response. I wasn't sure what to expect or what we would talk about.

But soon enough, Moji replied with the details of where and when to meet. I finished my breakfast with Wale cause we were soon going to see Moji.

As we drove to the meeting spot, my mind raced with memories of my childhood and teenage days with Moji. We had grown up together and were inseparable until I left for America. I wondered what she had been up to, and how she had changed. I know she married Kunle. I can't help but think about what we would talk about, will it be awkward?

When we arrived, I spotted Moji waiting for us. She had a big smile on her face and ran over to hug me.

"Femi! It's so good to see you," Moji exclaimed.

"You too, Moji," I replied, hugging her back. "It's been too long."

Wale and Moji exchanged pleasantries before leaving us to catch up.

Wale excused himself to give Moji and I some privacy, he left us alone at the table. I couldn't help but notice the wedding ring on Moji's finger. I knew she was married, but he still felt a dart of disappointment.

Moji noticed the expression on my face and said, "I know what you're thinking, Femi. But yes, I got married."

I forced a smile and said, "I'm happy for you, Moji. How's married life treating you?"

Moji sighed and said, "It's been a rollercoaster ride. There are good days and bad days, you know how it is."

I acted surprised that I didn't know Moji was married to Kunle. I couldn't believe that she married the same guy she had been dating on and off since high school. "Kunle? The same Kunle you used to talk about all the time?" I asked, my voice laced with disbelief.

Moji nodded, looking down at her lap. "Yes, Femi. I know it's a lot to take in. We got married a few years ago and got married this year," she said softly.

I sighed and leaned back in my chair. "Wow. I had no idea. I'm sorry, Moji. I wish I had known."

Moji shrugged. "It's okay. I didn't really advertise it. I'm just glad we could catch up after all these years. So where are you staying? How long are you in Lagos for?"

I told her about the hotel I was staying at in Victoria Island and that I was planning to stay for a few weeks. We chatted for a while longer, catching up on old times and talking about our lives. But I couldn't help but notice that Moji seemed unhappy. There was a sadness in her eyes that I hadn't seen before.

"Is everything okay, Moji?" I asked gently.

Moji hesitated for a moment before responding. "To be honest, Femi, things haven't been great with Kunle lately. We've been having some problems."

I raised an eyebrow. "What kind of problems?"

Moji sighed. "It's just...I don't know. We've been together for so long, and sometimes it feels like we're not really...connected anymore, you know? We're just going through the motions. I thought marriage would make me happy, but it's just made me more miserable. Kunle is always working, and when he's not, he's with his friends. We barely talk or spend time together anymore."

I reached across the table and took Moji's hand, "I'm here for you, Moji. Always."

Moji smiled weakly, "Thank you, Femi. It means a lot to me."

Moji paused for a moment and looked at me expectantly. "What do you say, Femi? Will you come to Abuja with me?" she asked.

I hesitated for a moment. I knew that spending more time with Moji would only complicate things further. I still had feelings for her, and I didn't want to be the reason she cheated on her husband.

"Moji, I don't know if that's a good idea," I finally replied. "I mean, I don't want to come between you and Kunle."

Moji let out a sigh. "I know you're trying to do the right thing, Femi," she said. "But I need to get away from all of this. Even if it's just for a little while. And I want to spend that time with you."

I could see the desperation in Moji's eyes, and he felt torn. I wanted to help her, but I didn't want to betray my own values. "I don't know, Moji," I said, shaking my head. "I think it's better if we just... just stay away from each other."

Moji looked down, disappointment notched on her face. "I understand," she said softly. "I'm sorry for putting you in this position. I just thought...never mind."

I put my hand on hers, feeling a dart of guilt. "Hey, don't apologize," I said. "I'll always be here for you if you need me. But maybe it's better if we just take a step back for now."

Moji nodded, and we both fell silent for a moment, lost in our own thoughts. I wondered how things had gotten so complicated between us. I still cared for Moji, but I couldn't ignore the fact that she was married. I knew that I needed to tread carefully around her, lest I fall back into old patterns.

Eventually, we said our goodbyes and went our separate ways. I couldn't help but feel a sense of sadness as I watched Moji walk away. I hoped that she would find a way to work things out with her husband and find happiness, but I knew that it wouldn't be with me and it was better without me.

***

I sat in the back of the taxi, scrolling through my phone as the car made its way through the bustling streets of Lagos. I had just left Moji and was feeling a mix of emotions. Part of me was happy to have caught up with her, but another part couldn't shake the feeling that something wasn't quite right.

I decided to distract myself by texting Kemi. We had plans to explore a different part of Lagos that day, and I was eager to see where she would take me.

"Hey gorgeous, where are we headed today?" I typed out and hit send.

It only took a few seconds for Kemi to respond.

"I was thinking we could check out the Yaba market," Kemi replied. "Have you ever been there?"

I shook my head, even though Kemi couldn't see me. "No, I haven't. Sounds interesting, though."

"Great! I'll meet you at your hotel in an hour," Kemi texted back.

I smiled to himself as he put his phone away. I was looking forward to spending the day with Kemi and getting to know her better. But I couldn't help but wonder what would happen if I continued to see Moji. I knew it was a bad idea, but I couldn't deny that I still had feelings for her.

As the taxi pulled up to the hotel, I paid the driver and made my way to my room to wait for Kemi.

***

Kemi was a fantastic guide, and I couldn't have been more thrilled with her as my tour guide for the week. Each day, she took me to a new part of Lagos, showing me all the must-see places and introducing me to the different Lagos culture.

We visited the National Museum, where Kemi taught me about Nigerian history, art, and artifacts. We also took a stroll through the Lagos City Mall, where I got to try some traditional Nigerian dishes.

The next day, we visited the Lekki Conservation Center, where we went on a nature walk and saw monkeys, peacocks, and other wildlife. We also had a picnic in the park while enjoying the scenery.

On the third day, Kemi took me to the beach in Lekki, where we rented jet skis and had a thrilling adventure on the water. We also enjoyed a seafood dinner by the beach.

The following day, we visited Lagos Island, where Kemi showed me around the bustling markets and shops. We went back to the National Theatre, and this time we watched a play, *Omo Eko*.

On the fifth day, we went on a boat tour of Lagos, where we saw the city from a different perspective. We also visited the Nike Art Gallery and saw some amazing Nigerian art pieces.

On the final day, we visited the Olumo Rock, which is a natural wonder in Abeokuta, Ogun State. We climbed the rock and had a fantastic view of the city. We also enjoyed some local delicacies before returning to Lagos.

I was determined to show Kemi a good time after the visit to Olumo Rock. She had taken me around Lagos for a whole week, showing me the best places to eat, shop, and sightsee. I knew she deserved something special, so I made reservations at one of the best restaurants in Lagos.

As we walked into the restaurant, Kemi's eyes widened with awe. The decor was magnificent, with chandeliers hanging from the ceiling, and the sound of soft music filling the air. I held her hand as we were escorted to our table.

The menu was vast, and I ordered the best dishes for both of us. As we waited for our food, I asked Kemi about her life. I discovered that she had just graduated from the university with a degree in computer science and was trying to figure out what to do next, while waiting to be called to serve the country through the National Youth Service Corp.

I listened intently as Kemi shared her hopes and dreams. I was impressed by her ambition and drive. As the food arrived, I couldn't help but notice the smile on Kemi's face. The dishes were delicious, and we enjoyed each other's company as we ate.

After dinner, I took Kemi to a rooftop bar that overlooked the city. We sipped cocktails and talked for hours. I felt a strong connection with Kemi, and I knew that I wanted to spend more time with her.

I leaned in and whispered in Kemi's ear, "Let's go dancing." Kemi's eyes sparkled as she nodded in agreement. I took her hand and led her out of the restaurant.

As we approached the club, the sound of music grew louder, and the neon lights illuminated the dark street. The bouncer recognized me and welcomed us inside.

The club was packed with people of all ages and backgrounds. Kemi and I made our way to the bar, and I ordered two drinks. Kemi sipped her drink and closed her eyes, savoring the sweet taste.

I took her hand and led her to the dance floor. The DJ was playing a mix of Afrobeat and hip hop, and the crowd was jumping and grinding to the beat.

I pulled Kemi close, and we swayed to the rhythm. The music was loud, but we didn't care. We were lost in the moment, lost in each other's presence.

As the night wore on, we moved to the VIP section, where I ordered a bottle of champagne and continued to dance close in each other's arms.

I was stunned by what I was seeing, turned to Kemi and noticed that she was looking at me. "What's wrong?" she asked.

I hesitated for a moment, trying to find the right words to say. "That's Moji," I said, pointing in Moji's direction.

Kemi looked over, scanning the crowd until she spotted Moji. "Who is she?" she asked.

I took a deep breath, unsure of how to respond. "She's an old friend," I finally said. "I didn't expect to see her here."

"Do you want us to invite her over?" Kemi suggested.

I hesitated for a moment, considering whether to bring Moji over to our VIP section or not. I knew that it might cause some tension between them. On the other hand, I didn't want to leave Moji alone with the stranger she was with, especially since she appeared to be intoxicated.

After a moment of contemplation, I agreed with Kemi's suggestion and we both went over to Moji's table. As we approached, Moji's eyes lit up in surprise and a hint of embarrassment flashed across her face.

"Hey, Femi," she said, trying to sound nonchalant. "What are you doing here?"

"We're just having a good time," I replied with a smile. "And we thought we'd come over and say hi."

Moji introduced them to her companion, who turned out to be a business associate. Kemi and I were polite and engaging, but we both sensed that Moji was uncomfortable and wanted to leave.

"Listen, Moji," I said, leaning in closer to her. "Why don't you come over and join us at our table? We have a VIP section, and I'm sure we can find a way to make you feel more comfortable."

Moji hesitated for a moment before nodding her head in agreement, she waved goodbye to the guy she was with. "Where are you going?" The associate she was with said, angrily. Kemi and I led the way, and soon we were all seated comfortably in the VIP section, sipping on drinks and engaging in lighthearted conversation.

The DJ played one of Kemi's favorite songs and she pulled Moji up from where she was seated to dance together. I watched in excitement. I was happy to see Moji happy and having fun.
I soon joined them to dance, I was sandwiched between them. We ordered more tequila and champagne. It was a night full of drinks, smoking, dance, laughter, fun and drinks.

Later on, I turned to Kemi and said, "Thanks for being so understanding. I know it must have been weird for you."

Kemi smiled and shook her head. "It's okay, Femi. I trust you. And besides, I am having a good time tonight. That's all that matters."

The rest of the night was a blur.

Chapter Thirteen

I woke up to the sun peeking through the window blinds, illuminating the hotel room in a warm glow. As I slowly opened my eyes and looked around the room. The sun was shining brightly through the window, casting a warm glow on the bed where I lay. I noticed that I was in bed with Moji and Kemi, who were still fast asleep and tangled up in my arms.

I gently untangled myself from the two women and sat up on the edge of the bed, my head throbbing from the alcohol and the lack of sleep. I rubbed my head and tried to piece together the events of the night before.

***

I remembered drinking too much, dancing with Moji and Kemi at the club, and then coming back to the hotel room with them.

As soon as we got in the room, Kemi popped open a bottle of champagne while Moji searched for some music to play on her phone. We chatted and laughed, catching up on old times and sharing stories about life. I couldn't help but notice the way Moji kept glancing at me, and I wondered if she still had feelings for me.

As the night wore on, the three of us became increasingly drunk and giddy. We danced around the room, singing along to the music and taking silly photos. At one point, Moji grabbed my hand and pulled me close to her, whispering in his ear.

Kemi noticed and smirked at me, knowing exactly what was going on. She encouraged us to kiss, saying it would be hot. I felt a rush of desire, but also a sense of guilt. I knew I shouldn't be doing this with Moji, especially since she was married.

Kemi kissed Moji, I was trying so hard to hesitate but the alcohol and the mood in the room were too much to resist. I leaned in and kissed Moji, our lips meeting in a heated embrace. Kemi cheered us on before unzipping my pants and playing with my manhood.

The girls soon threw me on the bed and undressed me, my excitement could be noticed from my bulging manhood. I couldn't believe what was happening, "is this something that normally happens when I am with Kemi?" I thought to myself, this was with Moji and Kemi, who seemed just as pleased with the situation.

"This could be my life. The girl of my dreams and my Lagos queen," I thought for a second before Moji jumped on me and kissed me, while Kemi played with me manhood.

I soon stood up and took charge, thrusting Moji first and followed by Kemi.

The three of them indulged in our sexual desires, exploring each other's bodies and enjoying the moment.

The air was filled with the sound of our labored breathing, moans, and sighs of pleasure.

It was the most passionate and intimate experience I had ever had.

****

I woke up to the scents of Moji's perfume, I struggled to open my eyes but I could tell she was close, because I could smell her, I don't know why I could smell her, last night was still hazy, Kemi and I had so much to drink, a bottle of champagne and a bottle of tequila will do that to you, I don't remember how we got back to my hotel room but I remember working with to ensure Moji was covered on the couch, her sent shouldn't be this concentrated if she is on the couch cause it is in the other room, "did I fuck Moji?

Damn Femi if you can smell her this close, you definitely fucked her." I said to myself.

I shook my head, trying to clear my thoughts as I continued to struggle to fully wake up. When I finally opened my eyes, I looked over at the two women. I noticed that they looked peaceful, their breathing slow and even. Kemi was in front of me, while Moji was sleeping behind me. My heart skipped. I realized that I needed to leave soon; my flight back to San Francisco was at night, and I still had a lot to do before leaving.

I got up and tiptoed into the bathroom to watch my face and brush my teeth.
After I was done, I went back to the bedroom and found Kemi stirring awake. "Good morning," I said with a smile.

Kemi smiled back and stretched, her bare body exposed to the cool morning air. "That was a wild night," she said, her voice hoarse from sleep.

I nodded, trying to keep my mind from wandering to the previous night's events. "Yeah, it was," I said.

Moji stirred next, and I noticed that she looked a bit uneasy. I wondered if it was because of what happened last night. "Good morning, Moji," I said.

Moji smiled weakly and sat up, rubbing her eyes. "Morning," she said, looking around the room. "I should get going. Kunle will be wondering where I am."

I nodded, understanding the implications of what she said. I knew that I had to be careful not to hurt anyone, including myself. "Sure, I'll call you a taxi," I said, reaching for the hotel phone.

A taxi for Moji soon arrived and she said her goodbyes to me with a passionate hug.

"You know, I don't mind being a second wife to you, Kemi," Moji said as she hugged Kemi goodbye.

"I will be down to have you both as my wives," I licked my lips looking at both of them hug.

"I know you won't mind that at all. *Ole*," Moji said, jokingly!

We all laughed!

I ordered room service and enjoyed breakfast with Kemi, chatting and laughing about the previous night's events. I had to ask Kemi, what her version of what happened last night, she said we almost had a quickie at the club but we needed to make sure Moji was fine, Kemi said "I was about to sit on me in our section when she saw Moji almost falling from the chair, we called it a night, put Moji on the couch, where she fell asleep and then we jumped on each other, I don't think I got the chance to sit on you like I wanted to at club," Kemi got us aroused and in the mood again before my phone buzzed, we did have our quickie before going to Wale who was waiting for me downstairs.

As I hugged Kemi goodbye, I felt a pinch of sadness. I had grown fond of her company over the past week and was going to miss her. She promised to stay connected and to keep in touch. I nodded, knowing that it might not be easy with the distance and the different time zones.

After saying my goodbyes to Kemi, I headed downstairs to the hotel lobby to meet up with Wale.

We decided to spend some time at a bar on the beach to walk and talk. I bought a well known Lagos street food called "*bole*" a roasted plantain that comes with sauce and spicy chicken which I enjoyed with a drink.

After sometime we decided to walk back to the hotel, I agreed to the kickback deal.

As I waited for my taxi to the airport, I reflected on my time in Lagos. I had reconnected with old friends, explored the city, and even found myself in a few unexpected situations. I knew that I would miss Lagos but also looked forward to returning home to San Francisco.

***

My flight back to San Francisco was long and tiring, but I couldn't shake off the memories of my time in Lagos. The vibrant city, the warmth of the people, my parents and the experiences with Kemi showing me Lagos in its authenticity.

As the plane landed in San Francisco, I felt a sense of relief and excitement to be back home. He grabbed his bags and headed out of the airport, breathing in the fresh California air. The cool breeze felt refreshing after the heat and humidity of Lagos.

As I drove home, and reflected on my time in Lagos. I realized how much I missed it and how disconnected I had become from my roots. I promised myself to make more trips back to Lagos and to stay connected to my culture.

Once I got home, unpacked and settled in. I checked my phone and realized that I got an email from Kemi, thanking me for the amazing time we had together. She attached some of our pictures to the email and ended it with the hope that she hoped to see me again soon. I opened my laptop to read the email and responded. I smiled and replied, promising to keep in touch.

***

I walked into the conference room, where all my colleagues were already seated, and waiting for me. I looked around the table, seeing the curious and expectant faces of my team.

"Good morning, everyone," I said, taking my seat at the head of the table. "I'm glad to be back in the office."

"Welcome back, Femi," one of my colleagues said. "We're all looking forward to hearing about your trip."

I smiled, feeling a rush of excitement. "Well, I'm happy to say that it was a very successful trip. We signed some major deals in both London and Lagos."

The room erupted in cheers and applause.

"That's great news, Femi!" Cody exclaimed. "Can you give us some more details?"

"Of course," I said, pulling out my laptop. "Let me show you the presentation."

I went through the slides, detailing the various deals we had made and the potential revenue streams we could expect from them.

As I spoke, I couldn't help but feel a sense of pride and accomplishment. I had worked hard to make these deals happen, and it was rewarding to see my efforts pay off.

"Wow, Femi, this is amazing," another colleague said, looking impressed. "You've really outdone yourself this time."

I smiled. "Thank you. It was a team effort, and I couldn't have done it without all of you."

The meeting continued for a while longer, I answered questions and discussed the finer details of the deals. By the time it was over, I felt tired but satisfied. It was good to be my own boss, and I was excited to see what the future held for FemCo Enterprise."

***

My workday was finally over, and I was eager to catch up with Zeke and Cody. We made plans to meet up at our favorite bar, and I was looking forward to unwinding with a couple of beers.

As I stepped out of the building, I saw Zeke and Cody waiting for me on the sidewalk.

"Hey man, how was your first day back?" Zeke asked, giving me a pat on the back.

"Busy as always," I replied with a chuckle. "But I'm ready to relax now."

We made our way to the bar, taking a seat at a table near the back.

"Alright, spill it," Cody said, raising an eyebrow. "What personal details do you have for us about your trip?"

I grinned, took a sip of whiskey. "Well, let's just say it was quite an eventful trip."

Zeke leaned forward, intrigued. "Eventful how?"

I leaned back in my chair, feeling relaxed. "Okay, so first off, in London, I met this amazing lady named Amaka at my cousin's wedding. We hit it off right away, and we spent the whole weekend together. Tessa also lives in London, remember her? The girl from the club in Saint Tropez, let's say we continued from where we stopped at Saint Tropez. And in Lagos, I met this pretty little thing, her name Kemi, she was what I will call - the best. I am getting goosebumps by just thinking about her."

Cody whistled. "Sounds like a good time."

"It was," I agreed. "But then things got even more interesting when I went to Lagos."

The friends leaned in closer, their curiosity piqued.

"I met up with Wale and some old business associates, and we closed some pretty big deals for us, but then I also ended up spending some time with Moji."

"Moji? Is that the same Moji?" Zeke exclaimed. "How did that happen?"

"To cut the long story short, we all ended up hanging out together, and things got a bit wild. I thought something happened because I woke up to her on the bed but nothing happened, Thank God."

Cody shook his head, a grin on his face. "Only you, Femi."

We spent the rest of the evening drinking and chatting, I was regaling them with stories from my trip. It felt good to be back home, surrounded by friends, and I knew I had a lot of work to catch up on in the coming days. But for now, I was content to relax and enjoy the company of my closest friends.

***

I walked out of the bar, feeling a little buzzed from the drinks I had shared with Zeke and Cody. I got into my car and started the engine, driving off into the night towards my Oakland Hills home.

As I drove, my thoughts drifted back to my recent trip to London and Lagos. I couldn't believe how much I had accomplished in such a short amount of time. I was proud of myself and excited for what the future held for FemCo Enterprise.

But as I turned onto my street, my thoughts were interrupted by a familiar face. It was Karen, my neighbor, standing outside her house and staring at me with a cold, calculated gaze. I felt a shiver run down my spine.

I thought Karen would have forgiven me and moved on but she was still visibly angry with me over the incident with her daughter, her cold gaze said more words than a big textbook. "Andrea is a grown woman and can decide who she wants to have sex with," I thought to myself as flashes of me putting Andrea in sexual positions, and Andrea undeniably enjoying herself in my pleasurably handful thrust became too vivid for me.

I quickly pulled into my driveway and got out of the car. I walked towards the front door, trying to ignore Karen's gaze. But she continued to watch me, her eyes following me as I moved towards my house.

I couldn't shake the feeling of unease that settled in my stomach. I knew Karen was still seeking revenge, and I didn't know what she was capable of, so I had to be careful.

As I unlocked my front door and stepped inside, I felt relieved to be back in the safety of my own home. But I couldn't shake the memory of Karen's cold, and vengeful stare. I knew I would have to keep an eye on her and be careful around her from now on.

I walked into the house, feeling drained after the encounter with Karen. I tossed my keys on the kitchen counter and grabbed a bottle of water from the fridge, trying to shake off the memory of Karen's menacing stare.

As I leaned against the counter, my phone buzzed, and I saw a message from Maria.

"Hey, Femi! Are you back in town? Can I come see you this weekend?" the message read.

I smiled, feeling a surge of excitement. I hadn't seen Maria in weeks, and I was eager to catch up with her.

"Hey, Maria! Yes, I'm back in town. I'd love to see you. How about we grab dinner on Saturday night?" I replied.

"Sounds perfect! Can't wait to hear about your trip. See you then!" Maria replied.

I felt a sense of relief. Seeing Maria would be a nice break from the stress of work and it will probably help me feel settled back in the Bay Area. I made a mental note to make reservations at one of our favorite restaurants and to catch up on everything that had happened since the last time we saw each other.

As I settled into the couch, I scrolled through my phone, checking emails and social media feeds. But my mind kept drifting back to Karen and her daughter, Andrea. I couldn't shake the memories of our intimate moments, I had set it up as revenge for what Karen did during my housewarming party but somehow I knew I needed to figure out a way to move on from the past.

But for now, I pushed those thoughts aside and focused on my plans with Maria. A dinner with my sweet spicy Mexican girl was just what I needed to unwind after a long week.

***

Few days had passed and I needed to get back to my healthy routine. I checked my calendar to confirm the days I would normally run to start my routine again after my recent travel. On my start day, I got home early from work to get some rest and soon after hit the pavement, my sneakers pounding against the pavement as I ran through the rolling hills of Oakland. The sun was just beginning to set, casting a warm, orange glow across the sky. I had been running for a while, lost in thought, when I noticed someone I was about to overtake on the trail.

I turned my head as I was about to go past the person and saw it was Catherine, jogging beside me. I knew there was a chance I could run into her at this time, I was hoping to surprise her after my trip when I was back. We had run at this time together a few times before, hence why I decided to run at this time but I wasn't sure she still ran at the same time.

"Hey, Beautiful," I said, slowing down a bit to match her pace. "How's it going?"

"Hey you," a surprised Catherine said, smiling. "You are back! I'm doing well. How about you? How was your trip? When did you get back?"

"Which one do you want me to answer first?" I asked.

We laughed!

"It was great, thanks for asking," I continued. "We closed some big deals in London and Lagos."

"Wow, that's amazing," Catherine said, impressed. "You're always jetting off to exotic places."

I chuckled. "I wish it was a glamorous business trip, but it's mostly just meetings and negotiations."

Catherine laughed, and we fell into a comfortable rhythm, running side by side. We talked about work, our families, and the latest gossip in the neighborhood. It was like we didn't miss a day but we missed each other. We soon made it back to the neighborhood, I slowed down behind Catherine as she led the way back to her house.

As Catherine led me to her house, memories flooded back to me. I remembered the last time I was here, how we had spent the night together, and the morning after. I tried to shake off the thoughts as we entered her house.

Catherine headed straight to the shower to clean up and refresh herself. I sat at the kitchen table, feeling nervous and unsure of what was happening between us. I didn't want to invite myself to join her since I hadn't seen her in weeks, I wanted to ease back into things with Catherine, when she called out to me, "are you not going to join me?" from the shower, "she is a mind reader," I said, feeling my heart race.

I hesitated for a moment, unsure of how to proceed before answering that I was on my way. I got up from the kitchen chair and headed to the bathroom.

As I entered the bathroom, I could see Catherine's curve and a glimpse of her features through the shower curtain. She turned to face me, a small smile playing on her lips.

"Hey," she said, her voice echoing in the spacious bathroom.

"Hey," I said, feeling a little awkward, trying so hard to keep my eyes focused on her face. "You needed help with your back?" I played dumb.

Catherine nodded, turning around so that her back was facing me. I took a deep breath and reached out to touch her skin. My fingers grazed her spine, and Catherine let out a soft moan.

I pressed my fingers into the spot, feeling the tension in her muscles. Catherine let out a sigh of relief as I worked out the knots in her back.

As I massaged her back, I couldn't help but think about how much I wanted to be with Catherine. She did something to me that was different from what other girls offered, it was like she was in control and yet easily yielded it for me. I knew if I wanted to be with her I would have to give her something more stable. I decided to focus on the moment and enjoy the time I had with her and how she made me feel.

After a few minutes, Catherine suddenly turned around to face me, her skin flushed from the hot water. I couldn't help but stare at her beautiful body, admiring her beauty.

"Thank you," she said, her voice soft.

I nodded, feeling a little overwhelmed. "Of course."

We stood there for a moment, unsure of what to do next. But then Catherine reached out and took my hand, pulling me towards her.

"Stay with me," she whispered, her lips brushing against his.

I felt a surge of desire course through me, I licked my lips losing all sense of responsibility. My clothes were on the floor and within a blink of an eye I gave in to my desires as I stepped into the shower.

Catherine and I stood in the shower, and continued to kiss as we let the hot water run over their bodies.

The water felt good on our skin, we closed our eyes and let the tension melt away. We continued to explore each other kissing and caressing as we embraced and held each other tightly, feeling the warmth of their love. I kissed her neck, Catherine let out another soft moan, took soft breaths and smiled. She had been missing this since we last spent time together. She opened her eyes as soon as I turned her around against the wall in the shower and continued to kiss her neck, feeling all over her soft skin.

The water ran over our faces and bodies, and we felt the heat of our passion rising.
We made love in the shower, and it was the most amazing experience.

"More, more, don't stop, I missed you, I've missed this, I've missed us," Catherine's hand on the wall, the other on my body as she continued to receive my strokes in delight.

We stayed in the shower for a few more minutes, enjoying the feeling of the water on our skin and the warmth of our love and body against each other and soon after we turned off the water and stepped out of the shower.

I spanked her bottom as she stepped out of the shower, "Damn!"

Catherine's smile was visible to me from the mirror which was right across us, as we tried to stay dry. Catherine hugged my body tightly with her head on my chest.

"Are you okay?" I hugged her back as our naked bodies kept each other company.

"Hmmm Hmmm," she murmured back at me, her voice barely heard.

I was smiling. I looked at myself in the mirror with satisfaction. That turned me on, I could feel my manhood bulging, so I guided her to the bedroom.

We made love a few more times before I kissed her forehead and left for my house.

As I arrived at my house, I saw a light brighten up the street. I looked back out of curiosity and saw that it was Karen, looking at me from her room upstairs letting me know she was still watching him.

"Oh my God, this woman won't stop," I said to myself as I entered the house.

***

Catherine's hands tightened on the steering wheel as she watched the unknown woman walking to my house. Who was she? And why was she going to Femi's house?

Her heart was pounding with jealousy and insecurity as she drove to her house. She quickly parked the car and rushed inside, slamming the door shut behind her.

She took a deep breath and tried to calm herself down. But the thought of another woman going to my house was too much for her to bear. She needed to talk to someone, and her friend Ariana was the perfect person.

Catherine grabbed her phone and dialed Ariana's number. After a few rings, Ariana picked up.

"Hey *babes*, what's up?" Ariana asked.

"I just saw some random woman going to Femi's house," Catherine said, her voice laced with jealousy. "I don't know who she is, but I don't like it."

"Wait, slow down," Ariana said. "Who's Femi, and why are you so upset?"

Catherine took a deep breath and tried to calm herself down. "Femi is the guy I've been seeing. I've told you about him before."

"Oh, right, him," Ariana said. "And who was this woman?"

"I don't know," Catherine said. "Some random woman. She was dressed up, and she was carrying a bag. I don't know what's going on."

"Maybe she's just a friend," Ariana suggested.

Catherine scoffed. "Yeah, right. A friend who goes to his house on a Saturday afternoon? Please."

"Okay, okay, I get it," Ariana said. "Didn't you say you were going to stop seeing him because you wanted something more stable, Catherine. You said you wanted things to progress between you and Jamal."

Catherine sighed. "I know. I'm just so jealous. I can't help it. I saw him on Thursday and the feelings came back, girl, he got to my bottom."

"Girl, you mean he got to your bottom? Like your Vijay bottom? My friend has been screwed to submission, your brain has been rewired, I get it now," Ariana said, laughing.

Catherine smiled, putting her groceries in her fridge. "Girl, I remember hugging him tightly and realizing that I don't own myself and I would do anything he wanted whenever and wherever."

"I get it, you do need a reset if you don't want to feel like this. Jamal maybe?" Ariana said. "Just remember, communication is key."

"Jamal is a two minute man, I had to finish myself, and that was the last time we got intimate," Catherine paused. "I'm screwed! I need to know who this girl is, I will text him tomorrow."

"Clearly Jamal can't help you and if you're really worried, just talk to Femi about it," Ariana said.

Catherine nodded. "You're right. I should talk to him. Thanks, Ariana."

"Anytime, girl," Ariana said. "Just remember, communication is key."

Catherine hung up the phone and took a deep breath. She knew Ariana was right. She needed to talk to me and get some answers. But for now, she just needed to calm down and relax.

***

Maria was wearing a deep red dress that hugged her curves in all the right places. Her long brown hair was styled in loose waves that cascaded down her back, and she wore minimal makeup that highlighted her natural beauty. I couldn't help but stare at her, struck by how beautiful she looked.

"Wow, Maria, you look incredible," I said, a genuine smile spreading across my face.

Maria grinned back at me. "Thank you, Femi. It's good to see you."

"It's good to see you too," I said, stepping closer to her. "I've missed you so much."

"I've missed you too," Maria said, leaning into me for a hug. We held each other tightly for a moment, reveling in the warmth of each other's embrace.

When we pulled away, I motioned for Maria to take a seat on the couch. "Can I get you something to drink?" I asked.

"Water is fine, thank you," Maria replied, settling onto the couch.

I headed to the kitchen to grab a bottle of water, my mind racing with thoughts of Maria. I couldn't believe how much I had missed her in the weeks since I had left for London and Lagos. As I handed her the bottle, I couldn't help but feel a surge of excitement at the thought of spending time with her again.

"So, tell me all about your trip," Maria said, taking a sip of water.

I launched into a detailed account of my travels, recounting my experiences in London and Lagos with enthusiasm. Maria listened intently, hanging on his every word.

As we talked, I couldn't help but notice that Maria came in with grocery bags. "What's in the grocery bags?"

"It is a surprise, I can't tell you, I will have to show or you'll have to see it yourself," Maria stood up, she slid into one of my flip flops, picked up the last grocery bag close to the door and headed to the kitchen.

"Surprise? This is going to be good." I walked towards Maria, I saw her removing stuff from the bags, I picked a bottle of water and left Maria alone to watch the game on TV.

I watched Maria as she bustled around the kitchen, slicing vegetables and pounding spices with deft movements. The aroma of the food wafted through the air, making his stomach growl in anticipation.

"What are you making?" I asked, standing up from the couch and walking over to the kitchen island.

"Jollof rice, moi moi, and pepper soup," Maria replied, grinning at me. "I figured you'd been missing Nigerian food."

My face lit up. "You're the best, you know that?"

Maria laughed. "I try my best."

As Maria continued cooking, I settled back onto the couch, turning on the TV to watch a basketball game. The sounds of the game mingled with the sizzle of the food in the kitchen, creating a cozy atmosphere that made me feel content.

When Maria finished cooking, she brought over a big plate of jollof rice, moi moi, and a bowl of pepper soup. I took a bite of the rice and moaned in delight. "This is amazing," I said between bites.

Maria beamed at me. "I'm glad you like it. I've been practicing."

We spent the rest of the evening watching movies, snuggled up on the couch. I felt happy and relaxed, grateful to have Maria back in his life.

As we got ready for bed, I turned to Maria. "Now it's my turn to give you some sweet chocolate dessert. Tonight I am serving you churros dipped in chocolate." I leaned in and kissed Maria passionately, I pulled away from her for a second and said in a low tone, "I missed you, you know."

Maria smiled. "I missed you too, Femi. It's good to have you back."

I stood up, "let me feed you these churros upstairs," I pulled Maria's hand gently to get her to stand, she resisted jokingly, when she stood, she ran up.

"You'll have to catch me first," Maria ran up the stairs into my bedroom.

I shook my head, smiled and ran after her.

I walked into my bedroom and found Maria seated at the edge of the bed, with only lingerie on. She posed like she was in her lingerie photoshoot, her hair on the side of her face, her lips slightly pouting, her voluptuous on display, her curves, thighs with her legs slightly opened.

She signaled me to come to her. I walked past her dress and shoes as I walked towards her. Maria opened her legs as soon as I got close to her, which gave me space to walk in.

I used my legs to spread hers further before leaning in to kiss her waiting lips. Our kiss soon turned passionate, I pushed her on the bed before going on top of her to continue to explore her body, I knew exactly how to touch Maria and what she wanted and how to give it to her.
Maria and I lay in bed, our bodies entwined. We had been making love for hours, and we were both exhausted and satisfied.

I kissed Maria's face followed by her forehead, and she smiled up at me. "That was amazing," she said.

"I know," I said. "I've never felt anything like it."

We lay in silence for a few minutes, just holding each other. Then Maria spoke.

"I love you," she said.

"I love you too," I said.

We kissed again, and this time it was even more passionate than before. We made love again, and this time it was even more intense than the first time.

When we were finished, we lay in bed, our bodies cuddled up. We were both covered in sweat, but we didn't care. We were happy and content.

Maria laid on my chest, she could hear my heartbeat as blood was pumping through it. I raised her chin up, we kissed again, and then we fell asleep in each other's arms.

"I'm pregnant, Femi, I am carrying your child," Maria said faintly.

I could hear her in my sleep but I was so deep in my sleep that it felt like I was dreaming.

"She told you she loved you and that she was pregnant with your child, how did you end up here?" My bunkmate, James, asked me.

Chapter Fourteen

"Trapped, It's a Wrap."

My heart raced as I heard the loud banging on my door. I rushed to the window and saw flashing blue and red lights outside. I could hear the sound of sirens getting louder as the police vehicles pulled up in front of his house.

"What's going on?" Maria turned when she heard me distraught, pacing in the room.

Without hesitation, I quickly made my way to the door and opened it. I was met by a group of police officers, all standing on my porch, guns drawn and pointed at me.

"Put your hands up!" one of the officers barked.

I complied, slowly raising my hands in the air. Another officer approached me and handcuffed me tightly, painfully digging into my skin.

"You're under arrest for criminal threats and domestic violence," the officer announced, reading me my rights.

I couldn't believe what was happening. I had never been in trouble with the law before. I tried to explain myself, but the officers were not interested in hearing it.

Maria was shocked and confused as she watched the police take me away in handcuffs.

As they led me outside, I could see my neighbors gathered outside, Karen included, watching in shock as I was escorted to the police car. The embarrassment and shame were overwhelming.

"This is probably Karen, she had been watching me for a while but on counts of criminal threats and domestic violence? That can't stick. Did she convince Andrea to file charges against me?" Multiple questions hit me at once as I tried to figure out what these charges were about.

I was taken to the police station, where I was fingerprinted and booked. I was placed in a holding cell with other criminals, feeling scared and alone.

I couldn't stop thinking about what had happened. I knew I had never threatened or harmed anyone. I wondered who could have accused him of such heinous crimes. I knew I needed to clear my name and get to the bottom of this.

***

"Whoop! They got you now!" James exclaimed!
"They sure did," I responded.

I sat in the cold and damp holding cell, my mind racing with thoughts about what could have led to my arrest. I couldn't believe that I was being accused of domestic violence and criminal threats. As I sat there, I started to think more about Karen.

I remembered the way she had been stalking me and how she had threatened me in the past. I wondered if Karen had somehow framed me and if the police had fallen for her lies. I tried to shake off the thought, but it kept nagging at me.

I thought about Maria and how she must be worried sick about me. I wished I could talk to her and tell her that I was okay, but I knew that wasn't possible at the moment. I felt helpless and trapped, and the more I thought about it, the more I believed that Karen had something to do with his arrest.

One thing was sure, I knew I had to get out of here and clear my name. I had to prove my innocence and find out who was behind this. I closed his eyes and took a deep breath, trying to calm myself down. But my mind kept going back to Karen, and I couldn't shake the feeling that she was somehow involved.

Zeke picked up the phone on the third ring, and Maria immediately launched into her story. She spoke quickly, her words tumbling out in a rush as she explained what had happened. Zeke listened patiently, his brow furrowed in concern as she described the events of the day.

After she had finished, there was a long pause on the other end of the line. Maria held her breath, waiting for Zeke's response.

Finally, he spoke. "Okay, Maria, listen to me. This is what we planned for. Everything is going to be fine."

Maria let out a shaky breath, relieved to hear his calm voice. "But what if something goes wrong? What if they find out that we set him up?"

Zeke's voice was firm. "That's not going to happen. We covered our tracks. Besides, we did this since we both know Femi wasn't going to marry you and now that you are pregnant for him. It was easier this way, you and your baby will be taken care of."

Maria nodded, feeling a sense of reassurance wash over her. "Okay. You're right. Thank you, Zeke."

"Of course," he replied. "Now, you need to get some rest. We'll talk more tomorrow."

Maria hung up the phone and collapsed onto her couch, feeling exhausted and drained. She couldn't shake the feeling of fear that had settled deep in her chest, but she knew that she had done the right thing. She just hoped that everything would work out in the end.

***

Zeke sat on his couch, a tumbler of whiskey in hand, as he let out a contented sigh. The random girl he had brought home from the bar sat next to him, looking at him with curiosity.

"Why are you so happy?" she asked, taking a sip of her own drink.

Zeke chuckled, and took another sip of whiskey. "Just got some good news, that's all."

The girl raised an eyebrow. "Wanna share?"

Zeke grinned, setting his glass down and turning to her. "Not really. But I could use a massage."

The girl smirked, putting down her drink and beginning to rub his shoulders. Zeke closed his eyes, enjoying the sensation.

As the girl worked her hands over his back, Zeke pulled out his phone and dialed his dad's number. After a few rings, his dad picked up.

"Hello?"

"Dad, it's me. The trap has caught the mouse," Zeke said, trying to keep his voice low so the girl couldn't hear.

His dad let out a small chuckle. "Good work, son. I'll make sure the lawyers are ready."

Zeke grinned, feeling a sense of satisfaction wash over him. "Thanks, dad. I couldn't have done it without you."

He hung up and turned back to the girl, taking another sip of whiskey. Everything was falling into place, and he couldn't be happier.

Zeke pulled the girl to come sit on his lap, he started caressing and kissing all over her body while undressing her. He had undressed her and started thrusting her from behind, doggy style when his phone started buzzing. He ignored, nothing was going to stop him from enjoying his celebratory sex. He had increased his thrusting tempo, he ignored the girl's displeasure, and her request for him to slow down.

"You are a fucking maniac," she said as she collected her clothes and left him on his couch where he was seated.

Zeke's phone rang, interrupting his thoughts. He picked it up and saw that it was a collect call from the Alameda holding cell and correctional center. He hesitated for a moment before accepting the charges, waiting to confirm, it was me on the other line.

"Hold up now, how did you know he had a girl there and he was fucking her?" James asked.

"Because he told me, fool," I responded and we both laughed.

"Hello?" Zeke said, cautiously, acting unaware of my arrest.

"Zeke, it's me, Femi," came the voice from the other end of the line.

"Femi! What happened? Are you okay?" Zeke asked, his heart smiling with joy but his voice portrayed differently, he sounded concerned.

I told Zeke what had happened and how I ended up in jail. Zeke listened intently, trying to figure out what to do next.

"I need you to call the lawyer from FemCo and get me out of here, Zeke. I can't stay in this place," I pleaded.

"Don't worry, man. I'll make the call right away. Just hang tight," Zeke said, trying to reassure me as a friend.

After hanging up the phone, Zeke pumped his fist in the air and did a celebratory dance before he dialed the number of the FemCo lawyer and explained the situation. The lawyer promised to do everything in his power to get me out of jail as soon as possible.

Zeke took a deep breath and leaned back in his chair, feeling the weight of the situation settle heavily on his shoulders. He couldn't believe that I was finally in jail, and he couldn't shake the feeling that his plan was finally working and being in control of the whole situation.

Nevertheless, he knew that he needed to stay focused and do whatever it took to own FemCo and destroy me.

***

Catherine had been thinking about me all morning as she got ready for church. She had planned to stop by my house after church and take me to brunch to talk about our relationship, especially now that she saw a lady in red walking towards my house. As she drove down the familiar route to my house, she saw the police cars parked outside and a sense of dread washed over her.

She parked her car and walked up to the front door, but there was no answer. She tried calling my phone, but it went straight to voicemail. Catherine knew something was wrong, and she started to worry that I might still be in jail.

She hesitated for a moment, wondering if she should go to the police station and try to see him. But she knew she had to attend church, and she didn't want to be late. Catherine made a decision to go to church first and check on me after the service.

As she sat in church, her mind wandered, and she couldn't focus on the sermon. She kept thinking about me, sent me a text, but got no response and wondered what might have happened. Catherine silently prayed that I was okay and that everything would work out.

After the service, Catherine hurried back to her car and drove straight to my house. There was still no answer so she headed to the police station. She asked the officers at the front desk if I was in custody. They confirmed that I was and gave her instructions on how and what she needed to do to see me.

"This is why I only fuck with older fine wine like her," James interjected.

"Can I finish the story bro?" I said, my hands gestured to emphasize that as well.

James nodded.

So, Catherine followed the instructions, and after going through security and waiting for what felt like an eternity, she finally saw me. She was relieved to see me but saddened by the conditions of the holding cell.

I explained what had happened, and Catherine listened intently, promising to help in any way she could. She offered to contact a lawyer to help bail me out. We made plans to talk more about the situation once I was released.

Catherine stepped out of the holding cell and quickly dialed Jamal's number. After a few rings, Jamal picked up the phone.

"Hey, Catherine, what's up?" Jamal said.

"Jamal, I need your help," Catherine said, her voice shaking. "Femi has been arrested and is being held at the Alameda correctional center. I need you to help bail him out."

"Whoa, slow down," Jamal said. "What happened? Who is Femi?"

Catherine hesitated for a moment when Jamal asked who I was. She knew that she had been seeing both men at the same time, and the truth would cause problems. So, she diverted and lied, saying that I was a friend who needed help. She told him that I had been arrested for criminal threats and domestic violence and that I needed a lawyer to bail him out.

"I'll see what I can do," Jamal said. "I have some connections at the Alameda courthouse. I will make a few calls first thing tomorrow morning, and I'll get back to you." He reminded her that today was Sunday, and the courts were closed, meaning that I wouldn't be able to get out until tomorrow, Monday.

Catherine sighed and thanked Jamal for his help, knowing that I would be grateful. She hung up the phone and felt a bit of guilt for lying to Jamal. She knew she had to figure out what she wanted and whom she wanted to be with.

***

I sat in the holding cell, feeling frustrated and helpless. I had hoped that the FemCo lawyers would be able to bail me out, but their efforts had been in vain. When they informed me that I would have to spend the night in the cell, I let out a deep sigh.

"Is there anything else we can do for you, Mr. Williams?" one of the lawyers asked.

I shook my head. "No, I guess not. Thank you for coming, though."

The lawyers nodded and left, leaving me in the cell once again. I leaned my head back against the wall and closed my eyes, trying to think of a way out of this mess.

As I sat there, I couldn't help but wonder how I had ended up in this situation. I had never been in trouble with the law before, and now I was facing criminal threats and domestic violence charges.

I knew that I needed to get out of jail as soon as possible and clear my name. I just hoped that I would be able to do so before it was too late.

***

I sat in the courtroom, my hands shaking as I waited for my arraignment. I was surrounded by other inmates, all waiting for their turn in front of the judge. The FemCo lawyers sat next to me, looking through their paperwork and occasionally whispering to each other.

Finally, my name was called, and he stood up, walking to the front of the courtroom. The judge looked down at me, and I felt a sense of dread wash over me.

The FemCo lawyers quickly spoke up, asking for bail for their client. But the defense lawyers argued that I was a flight risk, pointing to my Nigerian nationality and my extensive travel records.

"He has no ties to this community, Your Honor," the defense lawyer said. "And with his financial resources, he could easily flee the country."

My heart sank as I listened to the argument. I knew that I wasn't a flight risk, that I had no intention of running away. But I couldn't argue with the evidence presented by the defense.

The judge deliberated for a few moments before finally ruling in favor of the defense. "Bail is denied," he said. "The defendant is a flight risk, and there is a risk to public safety if he is released at this time."

"That's bullshit dog, you are a first time offender and had a company to run, that is just pure racist bullshit bro," James interjected again feeling obviously agitated.

"I know bro," I looked at him and I remembered how I felt then.

I hung my head as I was led back to my holding cell, feeling the weight of the charges against me and the impossibility of my situation. I sat there staring blankly ahead, lost in my thoughts. I couldn't believe what had just happened in court. The judge had denied bail, and I was now waiting to be moved to a correctional center. I replayed the events in my head, trying to make sense of it all. How did it come to this?

I noticed Zeke, and Cody sitting in the court, and I caught a glimpse of Karen watching me. I continued to wonder if Karen had something to do with my arrest. She had always been hostile towards me, but I couldn't imagine her going to such extremes.

As I sat there, I also couldn't help but wonder where Maria and Catherine were. I had expected them to be there to support me, but they were nowhere to be seen. I couldn't help but feel alone and abandoned.

I let out a deep sigh and leaned my head against the cold metal bars of the cell. The cell was small and cramped, barely big enough for one person. The walls were made of cold, gray concrete, with no windows to the outside world. The only source of light was a dim fluorescent bulb on the ceiling, which flickered incessantly.

The air was thick with the smell of sweat, urine, and other bodily fluids. The bed was nothing more than a thin mattress on a metal frame, with a scratchy woolen blanket that barely kept out the chill. The toilet was a metal bowl in the corner of the cell, with no privacy whatsoever.

The noise was deafening, with inmates yelling and shouting at each other, banging their fists against the walls, and sometimes even fighting. The guards were indifferent, just doing their jobs and not caring about the suffering of the inmates.

The worst part of the cell was the feeling of hopelessness that permeated everything. There was no way out, no escape from this nightmare. Days could easily turn into weeks, and weeks turned into months. It was a living hell, and the thought of spending the rest of one's life in such a place was enough to drive anyone insane.

I knew I had to stay strong and not lose hope, but it
was hard not to feel defeated in this moment.

I sat on the bed in my cell, feeling dejected and
helpless. I had been trying to reach Catherine for
days, but she had not been answering my calls. Finally,
after what seemed like an eternity of waiting, she
picked up the phone.

"Femi, how are you?" Catherine's voice sounded
tense, and I knew something was wrong.

"I'm okay, Catherine. I just wanted to check in and see
if you had any updates on my case."

There was a pause on the other end of the line, and I
could hear Catherine taking a deep breath.

"Jamal couldn't get you out on bail, Femi. He tried,
but his connection mentioned that the prosecutor's
names were sealed. We don't know who's behind this,
but we'll keep trying."

I felt a lump form in my throat. I couldn't believe that
I was still in jail, and now it seemed like I was up
against someone with a lot of power.

"I don't know what to do, Catherine. I feel like I'm
just stuck here, and I can't even fight back."

"I know, Femi. But you have to be strong. We're all here for you, and we'll do whatever we can to help."

I sighed. I appreciated Catherine's words, but I couldn't shake the feeling that I was all alone in this.

"Thanks, Catherine. I appreciate it. Please keep me updated if you hear anything."

"I will, Femi. Take care of yourself."

Catherine told me my next court date. I hung up the phone and lay down on the bed, staring up at the ceiling. I felt like I was in a nightmare that I couldn't wake up from. The thought of spending another day in jail was almost too much to bear.

***

Almost a month has passed, and I was still in the correctional center. The days were long, and I had lost track of time. I was no longer the CEO of FemCo, and I wondered what had happened with the company. I had been thinking a lot lately, and I knew I had to be strong to get through this. I had lost everything I had worked so hard to build.

One day, a guard came to my cell and informed me that I had a visitor. I was surprised and wondered who could be visiting me. I was escorted to the visitor's area and saw Zeke waiting for me.

"Hey man," Zeke said as he stood up to greet him. "How are you holding up?"

I was surprised to see Zeke, especially since he was now the CEO of FemCo. "I'm doing okay," I replied, trying to mask my surprise.

"I'm sorry about what happened," Zeke said. "I wish there was more I could have done to help."

"It's not your fault," I replied. "I appreciate you coming to see me."

Zeke nodded. "I wanted to let you know that the board has backed me, and I am now the new CEO of FemCo."

I was surprised but not shocked. I had expected it. "Congratulations," I said.

Zeke smiled. "Thanks, man. I promise to do right by the company and by you."

I knew Zeke meant well, but I couldn't help but wonder what was next for me. I had lost everything, and I didn't know where to go from here.

***

I woke up to the blaring sound of the intercom announcing that it was time to get ready for my arraignment. I rubbed my bleary eyes and took a look around the cell. The small space was dimly lit, and the air was thick with the smell of sweat and fear.

I got up from the bed and went to the sink to splash some water on my face. I had a shower yesterday, I am not going there today before something bad happens or someone tries to cut me just because, I thought to myself as I looked in the mirror, and my reflection showed the toll my time in the correctional center had taken on me. My once neat and clean-shaven appearance had been replaced by a scruffy, unkempt look. My clothes were wrinkled and stained, and my hair was matted and uncombed.

I quickly got dressed in the only set of clothes I had, a faded orange jumpsuit, and made my way to the door. The guard opened the door, and I stepped out into the dimly lit corridor. I joined a line of other inmates, all dressed in orange jumpsuits like me, shuffling towards the courthouse.

As I walked, I couldn't help but wonder what the day had in store for me. Would I be able to prove my innocence and get out of this hellhole, or would I be sent back to this cell to rot away for God knows how long? The uncertainty of it all was overwhelming, and I couldn't help but feel a deep sense of dread in the pit of my stomach.

***

All the inmates were allowed to change into presentable clothes. My lawyer had brought me some options for me to put on before going into the courtroom. I stood in front of the judge as my lawyer presented my case. I scanned the courtroom, and my heart leaped with joy as I saw his mom, Peju, sitting in the front row. She had flown all the way from Nigeria to be with me. I felt a mixture of emotions; I was happy to see her, but I also felt guilty for putting her through this ordeal.

As my lawyer continued to argue my case, I noticed Catherine sitting a few rows behind my mom. I felt grateful for her presence, even though I was not sure what our relationship was. I remembered how she had tried to help me with the bail, and I appreciated her efforts.

The judge interrupted my thoughts as he gave his ruling. My heart sank as I heard he denied my bail again and the case continued.

The prosecuting lawyers called their first witness. My heart sank as I watched Karen walk up to the witness stand. I couldn't believe my eyes. I had suspected her involvement in my arrest, but I never imagined that she would be a witness against me in court.

Karen took the oath and began her testimony. She recounted an incident where she had heard Femi shouting and threatening someone in his house. She claimed that she had heard him say things like "I'll kill you" and "I'll make you regret it."

I couldn't believe what I was hearing. I knew I had never threatened anyone, let alone said those words. I looked around the courtroom, hoping to find some support or evidence to counter Karen's claims.

My eyes landed on my mom, who was sitting in the front row, tears streaming down her face. I knew I had to stay strong for her. I took a deep breath and tried to gather his thoughts.

As the cross-examination began, My defense lawyer tried to poke holes in Karen's testimony. He asked her about the exact words I had used and whether she was sure it was me who had said them. But Karen remained firm and stuck to her story.

I could feel the weight of the situation pressing down on me. I knew that Karen's testimony could be the nail in the coffin for me. But I refused to give up. I turned to Catherine and my mom, who were sitting in the gallery, and gave them a small smile, silently assuring them that I was not going down without a fight.

The presiding judge looked sternly at the defense lawyers and announced that the case had been postponed to a future date, as they needed more time to review the evidence presented by the prosecution. Zeke arrived late and made his way to the defense table, where he whispered to the lawyers and asked them to confirm the situation. The lawyers nodded and whispered back that they needed more time to review the case and gather more evidence to prove my innocence.

I was relieved that the trial had been postponed, but I was also worried about what Karen's testimony would mean for my case. I felt betrayed that she could turn on me and lie like she did but I guess that was her way of paying me back for making her watch me and Andrea, flashes of Andrea giving in to my thrusting pleasure quickly flooded my memory but I had to quickly snap out of it. Karen is currently winning if this is how dirty she plays, I thought to myself.

My mom stood up from where she was sitting in the audience, walked over to me. "My son, are you okay? How are you holding up?"

I smiled and said, "I'm fine, Mom. Thank you for coming."

Catherine also walked over and said, "We'll keep fighting for you, Femi. Don't worry."

I nodded and said, "Thank you, Catherine. I appreciate it."

Zeke, on the other hand, seemed confident that they could win the case. He assured me that they would gather enough evidence to prove my innocence and get me out of the correctional center soon. I wanted to believe him, but the thought of spending another night in the cell made me doubt everything.

Catherine walked out of the courthouse with my mom, and offered her a ride back to my house. As they settled into the car, my mom couldn't help but ask about the case and Karen's involvement. Catherine shared the little information she knew about the case, assuring my mom that I was innocent.

As they drove, my mom looked at Catherine and asked, "What is your relationship with my son, Catherine?"

Catherine took a deep breath and replied, "We're just friends, Mrs. Williams. Femi and I have been friends for a while now, and I just want to help him in any way I can."

My mom nodded and looked out the window, lost in thought. "I just want him to be okay. He's been through so much already," she said quietly.

Catherine could sense the worry and fear in my mom's voice and tried to reassure her. "Don't worry, Mrs. Williams. We'll get through this. We'll do everything we can to clear Femi's name and get him out of there."

She nodded and looked at Catherine with gratitude. "Thank you, Catherine. Thank you for being there for my son."

Catherine smiled and said, "Of course, Mrs. Williams. Femi is my friend, and I'll do everything I can to help him."

As they pulled up to my house, Catherine helped my mom get out of the car. With her Nigerian motherly instincts, she looked around the neighborhood, taking in the scenery and making comments about the cleanliness of the streets until she noticed Karen standing in front of her house, staring at them. Her face bore a wide smirk, feeling satisfied with the chaos she had caused in court earlier, testifying against me in court.

In a stern tone, My mom said, "What do you find so amusing? Do you not have a heart? Don't you have any shame?"

Karen was taken aback by the sudden outburst and stuttered, "I...I don't know what you mean." She tried to defend herself, but my mom would hear none of it. She continued to scold Karen, reminding her of the pain and suffering she had caused.

Catherine tried to diffuse the tension by offering to take her inside, but Karen just stood there, looking at them before sipping her tea.

Karen watched as Catherine led my mom into the house, and a dark satisfaction settled in her heart. She had succeeded in getting me arrested and dragging my name through the mud. She couldn't help but revel in the fact that her plan had worked flawlessly.

My mom turned to Catherine and said, "Thank you and please, keep me updated on any news on Femi's case."

Catherine nodded and promised to keep her informed. As she watched my mom enter the house, Catherine couldn't help but feel the weight of the situation. She knew that my innocence needed to be proven, and she would do everything she could to help me.

Chapter Fifteen

"The Showdown."

The news of former FemCo's CEO on trial in Alameda County spread like wildfire across various news outlets and social media platforms. The sensational trial was the talk of the town, and people were speculating about my fate.

As the trial progressed, news updates flooded the internet, and people followed every development with bated breath. The media outlets tried to uncover every detail and piece together the puzzle of my case. Some claimed that I was innocent, while others speculated that I was guilty of the crime I was accused of.

The trial had become a national event, and the whole world was watching as I fought to clear my name. The stakes were high, and the outcome of the trial would have far-reaching consequences not only for me but also for FemCo.

As the trial dragged on, tensions rose, and the drama reached its climax. All eyes were on the courtroom, waiting for the next trial date that could potentially determine my future.

Amaka couldn't sit still after seeing the news of my trial on TV. She immediately reached out to Rebecca, to share her concerns. Rebecca tried to comfort Amaka and advised her to follow her heart.

"Amaka, you have to do what you feel is right. If you want to be there for Femi, then you should go. But please be careful and don't get too involved in his troubles," Rebecca said.

Amaka felt relieved after talking to Rebecca and decided to book a flight to San Francisco to support me. She also informed Rebecca that she was coming, and Rebecca promised to tell her husband, Bidemi, who was my cousin or step brother.

Rebecca knew Bidemi would be interested in hearing about my situation, so she wasted no time in letting him know. When Bidemi heard about my trial, he was shocked and saddened. He knew I had been going through a lot lately and hoped I would come out of it unscarred.

Bidemi decided to reach out to my family to offer his support and see if there was anything he could do to help. He knew that my mom would be devastated by the news, and he wanted to be there for her as well.

***

Catherine walked through the metal detector and handed her belongings to the security guard, who inspected them thoroughly before returning them to her. She then proceeded to the visiting room, where she took a seat at one of the tables and waited for me to arrive. The room was dimly lit and had a cold, sterile feel to it. The walls were painted a dull gray, and the only decoration was a small, framed photograph of a scenic landscape.

As Catherine waited, her mind wandered to the last time she had seen me. I had been so hopeful, so confident that I would be able to beat the charges against me. But now, she could see the weariness in my eyes, and she knew that the past few weeks had taken a toll on me.

After what felt like an eternity, the door to the visiting room opened, and I was escorted in by a guard. I looked different from the last time Catherine had seen me - my hair was unkempt, and I had dark circles under my eyes. Despite this, Catherine was relieved to see me.

"Femi," she said, standing up to greet him.

"Catherine," I replied, taking a seat across from her. "I'm so glad to see you."

"How have you been?" she asked, trying to sound upbeat.

I let out a sigh. "It's been tough," I said. "But I'm hanging in there."

Catherine nodded sympathetically. "I'm sorry about everything that's happened," she said. "I wish I could have done more to help you."

I shook my head. "You've done more than enough," I said. "I don't know what I would do without you."

Catherine smiled weakly. "I'm just glad I can be here for you," she said.

"How's my mom? Have you heard from her? Do you know where she is staying?" Femi asked anxiously.

"Your mom is doing okay," she began, "but she doesn't want to see you in here. She's been worried sick about you."

I sighed heavily, my eyes downcast. "I don't blame her," I muttered. "I never thought I'd end up in a place like this."

Catherine reached across the table and took my hand. "We'll get you out of here, Femi," she said firmly. "We just have to keep fighting."

I nodded, then asked, "Why do I get a feeling there is something else you want to tell me?"

Catherine hesitated for a moment before continuing, "There's something else you should know. Some girl named Maria has filed for domestic abuse against you. They say they have evidence of you abusing her."

My eyes widened in shock. "What? That's not true! Maria and I never had issues, and I never laid a hand on her."

Catherine nodded sympathetically. "I believe you, Femi. But we need to prove it in court. I've already spoken to Jamal, and he's working on it."

I sighed heavily and leaned back in the chair. "This is just getting worse and worse," I muttered. "I don't know how much more I can take."

Despite the bleak surroundings, Catherine found herself feeling hopeful. She knew that I was innocent, and she was determined to help clear my name.

***

I was surprised when the FemCo lawyers arrived at the correction center to see me. "Two visitors in a day? That's a record," I thought to himself.

I sat across the table from the FemCo lawyers in the correction center's visiting room. My eyes were sunken, and my face had lost its usual glow. The lawyers had just presented me with a plea deal, but I was hesitant to take it. I couldn't believe I was in this position, and I couldn't understand why Maria could have filed the charges against me.

"Do you know who filed these charges against me?" I asked, my voice shaky.

The lawyers looked at each other briefly before one of them replied, "I'm sorry, Mr. Williams, but the names of the accusers have been sealed. We don't have that information."

My heart sank. I couldn't believe that I was being accused of something that I didn't do, and I couldn't understand why the accuser, who could be Maria, would want to remain anonymous. I knew that I had to fight this, but I also knew that the evidence might be stacked against me.

The lawyers continued to press me to take the plea deal, but I was hesitant. I knew that by taking the plea, I would be admitting to something I didn't do. However, the lawyers argued that it was my best option, considering the evidence against me.

After much deliberation, I finally agreed to take the plea deal. As the lawyers left the visiting room, I sat there, my mind racing with thoughts of why the FemCo lawyers didn't have access to the information of who filed the charges against me. I knew that I had to find out the truth, but for now, I had to focus on getting through his sentence and clear my name.

"Get up, inmate, it's go time," the voice of a correction officer snapped me out of my thoughts.

I couldn't believe what I had heard from the FemCo lawyers, and my heart sank further as I realized that I might have to take the plea deal. I was devastated and felt like I had lost everything. I needed to talk to someone, anyone who would understand what I was going through.

"Was that when your sorry ass came running to talk to me?" James interjected again.

"I can't with, yes, that was when I came running to talk to you because you'd understand what I was going through, but not only you" I replied.

I couldn't wait to talk to someone during the call time set aside for us inmates to call our loved ones. After some time waiting on the line, I picked up the phone and dialed Zeke's number. When Zeke answered, I could hear the nonchalant tone in his voice. Zeke advised me to take the plea deal, saying that it was the best option for me.

I was shocked. How could Zeke be so casual about the whole thing? I was facing serious charges, and Zeke was acting as if it was just another business deal.

I tried to reason with Zeke, but Zeke wouldn't budge. He told me that I needed to think about the bigger picture, that he couldn't risk the company's reputation and shareholders' investments by fighting the charges in court.

I was angry and frustrated. I couldn't believe that Zeke was willing to sacrifice my life for the sake of the business I built from the ground up. I hung up the phone, feeling even more alone and helpless than before.

As I walked back to my cell, I couldn't help but wonder why Maria would have filed the charges against me. I had no idea she could have done such a thing, and it was driving me crazy not being able to reach her. She was there when I was arrested, she knew it was happening, I made love to her all night and it was all part of her plan.

***

Zeke called Maria to let her know that I was going to take the plea deal. Maria was happy to hear that, but Zeke didn't stop there. He revealed that he had a plan to take over FemCo permanently and offered Maria a chance to join him. Maria was hesitant at first, but Zeke assured her that he had everything under control and that it was the perfect opportunity to ensure I would never be able to come back and take the company from him. Maria eventually agreed to Zeke's plan, but she couldn't shake off the feeling of guilt for my situation.

Zeke smiled to himself as he hung up the phone. "Good," he said to himself. "Everything is going according to plan."

***

Amaka walked into the visiting room of the correctional center, wearing a serious look on her face. I was surprised to see her and asked what she was doing in California.

"I'm here for you," she replied, taking a seat across from me.

My face softened, and I looked grateful. "Thank you, Amaka. It means a lot to me."

Amaka nodded, then asked, "How are you holding up?"

I shook my head. "It's tough in here, but I'm trying to stay strong."

"I can only imagine," Amaka said sympathetically. "But I want you to know that I believe in you, Femi. You're not alone in this."

I smiled at her words, feeling a glimmer of hope. "Thank you, Amaka. I really appreciate your support."

We continued talking, catching up, and reminiscing about old times. Amaka also assured me that she would do everything in her power to help him, including finding out who was behind my current predicament.

After some time, I poured out my heart to Amaka, explaining my frustration with the FemCo lawyers and the plea deal they were pushing me to take. I told her how I felt that they were not giving me all the information I needed to make the best decision. Amaka listened intently, nodding and occasionally interjecting with words of encouragement.

When I finished, Amaka took a deep breath and looked me in the eye. "Femi, you have to do what's best for you. If you believe that Jamal can win this case for you in court, then you should fire the FemCo lawyers and hire him. Don't let anyone pressure you into a decision that you're not comfortable with."

I hesitated. "I don't know. I feel like I'm in too deep with these guys. And what if Jamal can't do anything either?"

Amaka shook her head. "Femi, you have to trust your gut. If you believe that Jamal can do a better job, then you should give him a chance."

I looked at her, considering her words. I knew she was right. I couldn't let anyone else make this decision for me. "You're right. I'll give Jamal a call and see if he's interested."

Amaka smiled. "Good. And Femi, I'm here for you. Whatever you need, I'll do my best to help you out."

I was grateful for her support. "Thank you, Amaka. It means a lot to me."

***

The morning at the FemCo office in San Francisco was a buzz of activity. Employees were bustling about, some chatting in groups, while others had their heads down, typing furiously on their keyboards. Cody sat at his desk, scrolling through his emails, trying to clear his inbox before the town hall meeting began.

As the time for the meeting drew closer, employees began to filter into the large conference room. There was a palpable sense of anticipation in the air, as everyone waited for Zeke to arrive. Cody could feel the nervous energy, and he wondered what Zeke had in store for them.

Finally, the door at the front of the conference room opened, and in walked Zeke, flanked by a group of executives. He strode confidently to the podium at the front of the room, and the crowd of employees fell silent, eager to hear what he had to say.

"Good morning, everyone," Zeke began, his voice carrying easily throughout the room. "I'm glad to see so many of you here today. We have a lot to cover, so let's get started."

Cody leaned forward in his seat, eager to hear what Zeke had to say. He knew that the past few months had been tumultuous for the company, and he was curious to hear what Zeke had planned for the future.

Zeke stood in front of the FemCo employees, addressing them as the new CEO. He presented the latest financial report, highlighting the company's successes in the past quarter. The numbers looked promising, and the employees cheered.

Zeke then shifted gears and addressed the elephant in the room, the situation with me. He reassured the employees that the lawyers were doing everything they could to get me out and that they were confident in their ability to win the case.

"We all know that Femi is the heart and soul of this company," Zeke said, his voice unwavering. "But we also believe that he is innocent, and we will fight to prove that in court. We are a family here at FemCo, and we stand by each other through thick and thin. And I promise you, we will come out of this stronger than ever."

The employees clapped and cheered in support, and Zeke felt a wave of gratitude and relief wash over him. He knew the road ahead would be tough, but with the support of the FemCo family, he was confident they could weather any storm when I took the deal.

What Zeke didn't tell his team was that he was in conversation to sell the company to another company who had been excited about the work done at FemCo and had approached me in the past to sell, which I declined.

Jamal Jackson, my new attorney, made a call to the prosecution team to let them know that his client had decided not to take the plea deal. He also confirmed the date for the next court appearance. The prosecution team, surprised by the sudden change in my decision, questioned Jamal about his strategy. Jamal explained that he believed they had a stronger case than the prosecution team had assumed and that they would be able to win in court.

Soon after the call, Jamal arrived at the correction center, where I was being held. After going through security, he was led to the visiting room where I was waiting for him.

"Hey man, good to see you," I said, shaking Jamal's hand.

"You too, Femi. How are you holding up?" Jamal asked.

"Not great, but I'm hanging in there," I replied, looking tired and stressed.

Jamal spoke to the prison officials and requested a conference room for him and I to review the evidence. After a brief wait, we were led to a small, windowless room with a table and chairs.

We sat together in the conference room, surrounded by stacks of papers and documents. Jamal had received the evidence from the prosecution team, and he had asked me to join him to review it.

We went through each document, analyzing the statements, the photos, and the videos. Jamal took notes, asked me questions, and made sure I understood everything.

As we went through the evidence, my face twisted in disgust and anger. I couldn't believe what I was seeing. I vehemently denied ever laying a hand on Maria, and I was determined to clear my name.

Jamal saw the determination in my eyes and nodded, "We have a good chance of winning this case. We'll go through every piece of evidence and find the truth."

I leaned back in my chair, relieved that I finally had someone on my side. "Thank you, Jamal. I'm ready to fight this and clear my name."

Jamal laid out the evidence on the table and began going through each piece with me, something the FemCo lawyers didn't do. As we reviewed the documents and witness statements, Jamal pointed out inconsistencies in the prosecution's case and potential areas of weakness. I listened intently, nodding in agreement and occasionally asking questions.

After the call, I felt relieved and grateful to have Jamal on my side. I knew I had made the right decision by hiring him.

***

As Zeke was sitting in his office, his phone rang. He picked it up and saw it was his dad calling. His heart sank a little, as he knew that his dad only called when something important was happening.

"Hey, Dad," Zeke said, trying to sound calm.

"Zeke, listen to me," his dad said urgently. "I just got a call from my *connect* in the prosecution team. Femi didn't take the plea deal. They're going to court."

Zeke felt his stomach drop. He had been hoping that Femi would take the deal and avoid a messy court battle that could drag on for months and potentially expose him and Maria. Now, it seemed like that hope was gone.

"What does this mean for us?" Zeke asked, trying to keep his voice steady.

"It means we're in for a fight," his dad said. "We have to do everything we can to protect the company, Zeke. This trial is going to be all over the news, and we can't let it tarnish FemCo's reputation till it's sold off. Don't forget to handle the girl, no loose ends."

"I know, Dad," Zeke said, feeling overwhelmed. "I'll do everything I can, I'll take care of it."

"I know you will," his dad said. "But Zeke, you have to understand that this is serious. We're talking about your future, that of the company so that we can sell it at a higher valuation. We can't afford to lose."

Zeke knew his dad was right. The stakes were high, and he couldn't afford to let my trial damage FemCo's reputation and he could lose everything as well. But he also couldn't help feeling a bit of sympathy for me, who he had grown up into a man with and considered a friend.

As he hung up the phone, Zeke knew that he had some tough decisions ahead of him. He had to protect himself, the company, but he also had to decide where his loyalties truly lay.

***

Maria walked into her apartment building and immediately noticed Zeke standing in the lobby. Her heart sank, knowing that something serious had happened.

"Zeke, what's wrong? Is everything okay?" she asked, rushing towards him.

"Maria, we need to talk," he said, leading her to a quiet corner of the lobby. "Femi didn't take the plea deal."

Maria's eyes widened with shock. "What? Why not? I thought he was going to take the deal and get a reduced sentence."

"He fired the lawyers from FemCo and hired some lawyer, Jamal Jackson, who convinced him that they have a chance to win the case in court," Zeke explained. "But this means that the trial is going forward, and it's going to be much more difficult for us to control the narrative."

Maria felt her world start to crumble. "What does this mean for me? Am I going to have to testify? I can't do that, Zeke. You know that."

"We'll do everything we can to make sure you don't have to go on the stand," Zeke assured her. "But we need to be careful. The prosecution team is going to be more aggressive now that Femi didn't take the plea deal."

Maria felt a surge of anxiety wash over her. She had never been involved in something like this before, and the thought of being dragged into a courtroom was terrifying.

"What do we do now?" she asked, looking up at Zeke with pleading eyes.

"We stick to the plan," he said firmly. "We keep pushing forward and doing everything we can to protect ourselves and the company. We can't let this setback stop us."

Maria took a deep breath, trying to calm her nerves. She knew Zeke was right. They had come too far to give up now.

"Okay," she said, nodding her head. "We'll keep going."

Zeke put a hand on her shoulder. "I'll be with you every step of the way, Maria. You're not alone in this."

Maria forced a small smile, grateful for Zeke's support. But she couldn't shake the feeling of dread that settled in the pit of her stomach. The trial was coming, and she wasn't sure she was ready for what was about to happen.

***

Maria's hands trembled as she clutched her phone, tears threatening to spill down her cheeks. She dialed Khadi's number and waited for her to answer. When Khadi arrived, Maria let her in and collapsed on the couch, her head buried in her hands.

"What's going on, Maria? What did Zeke say?" Khadi asked, sitting down next to her friend.

Maria took a deep breath and tried to compose herself. "He told me that Femi didn't take the plea deal," she said, her voice shaking. "I don't know what to do, Khadi. I'm scared."

Khadi put a comforting arm around her friend's shoulders. "Scared of what, Maria? You haven't done anything wrong. You just have to tell the truth."

"But what if they don't believe me? I am afraid," Maria asked, her voice barely above a whisper.

Khadi sat next to Maria on the couch and placed a hand on her shoulder. "Maria, why are you so afraid to take the stand? I know you love Femi and want to see him come home. If you testify and tell the truth, it could be the key to getting him acquitted."

Maria took a deep breath and looked at Khadi with a mixture of fear and sadness in her eyes. "It's not that simple, Khadi. You don't know what it's like to be in my position. I'm scared of what might happen if I testify. What if they try to make me out to be a liar or a criminal? What if they try to discredit me in some way? I don't know if I'm strong enough to handle it all."

Khadi squeezed Maria's shoulder reassuringly. "I understand that it's scary, but I believe in you, Maria. I know you're strong enough to do this. And think about Femi. He's counting on you to help him get out of this mess. You're carrying his child, and he needs you now more than ever. Don't you want to be able to look back on this moment and know that you did everything in your power to help him?"

Maria nodded slowly, tears welling up in her eyes. "Khadi, my testimony isn't going to help him come home." Her voice breaking.

Khadi adjusted herself on the couch, "what do you mean, your testimony won't help Femi come home?"

Maria stood up from the couch, her hands resting on her growing belly. Khadi listened intently as Maria recounted the story of the patient who died in their care at the hospital. "Zeke knows about it, Khadi," Maria said. "He's using it as leverage against me. He's

threatening to ruin my life, my career, basically
everything I've worked hard for if I didn't help him
bring Femi down."

Khadi's expression turned from confusion to
concern. "Maria, that's not right. You shouldn't have
to do this under duress. You have to tell someone."

"I can't," Maria replied. "I will have to mention that
you and the other nurses who are equally responsible
for Mr. Green's demise and personally, I have too
much to lose. My career, my reputation, and now with
the baby, I can't risk it all. I just wish Femi had taken
the plea deal. This is too much to bear."

Khadi looked scared, her eyes wide opened with her
hands placed on her chin. "I understand why you're
scared, Maria." She paused. "I am scared now as well,
Femi should have taken the plea deal, instead of us
facing eight years in jail."

Maria nodded, tears streaming down her face. "I
know, Khadi. I know. The fact that he didn't take the
deal is making things hard. It's really hard for me.
Femi has been calling me from the correction center
but I don't have it in me to talk to him or visit him."

"So what are you going to do, if you have to testify in
court?" Khadi asked.

"If I don't show up in court, Zeke is going to ruin me, I don't want to have my baby in jail. If I show up in court, the man that I love will be sent to jail for a longtime and will never forgive me. I don't know Khadi, I don't know." Tears continued to run down Maria's face.

Chapter Sixteen

"The End is Near, Fear Women."

Catherine arrived at the Soul Food Kitchen restaurant and exchanged pleasantries with Jamal. As they were seated, Jamal began to discuss the evidence he found and the strategy for my case. Catherine listened intently and asked questions when necessary. However, the conversation took a turn when Jamal asked Catherine about her relationship with Femi.

"When were you going to tell me about your relationship with Femi?" Jamal asked, a hint of accusation in his tone.

Catherine was caught off guard by the question. "I'm not sure what you're talking about," she replied, trying to play it cool.

"Don't play dumb, Catherine. I've seen the security footage from Femi's house. You've visited him several times," Jamal said, his voice rising.

Catherine felt a flush of embarrassment spread across her cheeks. "Look, Jamal, it's not like that," she said, her voice low.

"Then what is it like, Catherine? Are you dating him?" Jamal demanded.

Catherine hesitated before answering. "Yes, we've gone on a few dates. But it's nothing serious," she said, hoping to downplay the situation.

Jamal shook his head. "This is not good, Catherine. You're too emotionally invested in this case. I can't have that affecting your testimony on the stand," he said sternly.

Catherine sighed. "I am sorry, Jamal. It didn't mean anything to me, that is why I didn't mention it to you."

Jamal drank some water and shrugged. "I understand, I'm a professional, and I won't let my personal life interfere with my job. Now let's get back to the case. Is there anything else I should know about your relationship with Femi?"

"Nothing!" Catherine said with a small smile.

Jamal nodded. "Good. Now let's get back to the case."

***

As the date of my trial drew closer, tensions rose both in the San Francisco Bay Area and Lagos. News of the trial dominated the headlines in both cities, with reporters camped outside the courthouse in San Francisco and outside my family home in Lagos.

In San Francisco, news outlets speculated about the evidence that would be presented in court, with many wondering if the prosecution had a strong case against me. Some reporters speculated that my defense team may have uncovered new evidence that could change the course of the trial.

Meanwhile, in Lagos, my family and friends anxiously awaited news from San Francisco. Many held prayer vigils and rallies in support of me, hoping that justice would prevail.

The tension was perceivable on both sides of the Atlantic as the trial date approached. My fate hung in the balance, and the world was watching to see how the trial would unfold.

As the day of the trial finally arrived, crowds gathered outside the Alameda County Superior Courthouse in Oakland, while in Lagos, my supporters held a prayer vigil. The tension was at an all-time high, as everyone waited to see what would happen next.

***

The Alameda County Superior Courthouse was buzzing with anticipation as people flooded into the courtroom, eager to see what would happen in my case. The crowd was a mix of journalists, legal professionals, and curious onlookers.

The air was thick with tension and excitement as people waited for the trial to begin. The sounds of shuffling feet, whispered conversations, and occasional coughs echoed through the courtroom.

The seats were quickly filled, and people began standing along the walls and at the back of the room. The judge's bench was elevated above the rest of the room, and the prosecutor and defense attorneys took their seats at their respective tables.

The jury box was filled with potential jurors, and the judge's clerk began the process of selecting the final twelve jurors and alternates. The judge entered the courtroom to the sound of shuffling papers and quiet whispers.

As the judge took her seat, the bailiff announced the start of the proceedings, and everyone rose to their feet. The judge welcomed everyone to the trial, and the prosecutor began their opening statement.

The tension in the room continued to grow as the prosecutor laid out their case against me. The atmosphere was charged with emotion as witnesses were called to the stand and evidence was presented. The first witness the prosecutor called was Karen, my neighbor who had accused me of sexually harassing her daughter, Andrea. Karen took the stand and recounted how I had made inappropriate comments to her daughter while she was playing outside their home. She testified that I had said things like "you look pretty today" and "you're going to break a lot of hearts of these young boys." Karen also testified that she had seen me staring at her daughter in a lewd manner on several occasions.

During the cross-examination, Jamal asked Karen where she had witnessed me sexually harassing Andrea. He asked if it was from her room into my room where Andrea and I were having a good time, two consenting adults having sex. Karen appeared to be taken aback by Jamal's questioning, and her testimony started to crumble. Jamal then showed the jury videos of Andrea voluntarily visiting me at my house, further weakening Karen's testimony. The videos showed Andrea and I hanging out together and having a good time, which contradicted Karen's claim that I had harassed her daughter.

The tension in the courtroom rose as the videos were played, and the jury's attention was firmly fixed on the screen. My family and friends in the courtroom let out a sigh of relief as the videos cast doubt on Karen's testimony. The prosecutor attempted to counter Jamal's questioning, but it was evident that the damage had already been done.

As the cross-examination ended, the judge called for a recess, and the court adjourned for the day. Outside the courthouse, reporters were eager to interview Karen and Jamal, and the news of the videos quickly spread. The case had taken an unexpected turn, and everyone was eager to see how it would play out in the coming days.

Jamal stepped out of the courthouse and was immediately met by a swarm of reporters and cameras. He stood in front of the courthouse, taking a deep breath before he began speaking.

"Ladies and gentlemen of the press, I want to thank you for your interest in this case. I know it has been highly publicized, and emotions are running high. However, Femi's family would like the press to continue to respect their privacy during this difficult time."

Jamal paused for a moment, looking directly at the cameras. "Today was a good day," he continued. "We were able to challenge the testimony of the prosecution's first witness, Karen, and expose some inconsistencies in her story. We are confident that justice will prevail in this case, and we will continue to fight for Femi's innocence."

As Jamal finished his statement, the reporters continued to barrage him with questions, but he calmly walked away, knowing that his words had been heard. He hoped that the media would heed his call for privacy, but he knew that it was unlikely. Regardless, Jamal was focused on the task at hand, and he would not let anything distract him and his team from fighting for his client.

My family, Bidemi, and Amaka left the courthouse, all of them wearing dark glasses to avoid the flashing cameras of reporters who had been waiting for them outside. My parents walked silently, their faces imprinted with worry lines. My sister kept her eyes down, lost in her thoughts, while Bidemi and his wife, Rebecca, walked close together, their arms linked.

Amaka led the way to her car, and the others followed behind her in a tight group, as if they were protecting each other. As they reached the car, Amaka unlocked it with her remote, and they all piled in, grateful for the privacy that the car provided.

Once they were all inside, Amaka started the engine and pulled out of the parking lot, driving slowly to avoid any accidents. No one spoke at first, each lost in their own thoughts, replaying the events of the day in their minds.

Finally, my mother spoke up. "I can't believe they would say those things about my son. He's never been that kind of person."

My father reached over and took his wife's hand. "We know who our son is," he said. "We just have to trust that the truth will come out in the end."

Bidemi nodded in agreement. "Jamal did a good job today. He's going to get Femi out of this mess."

Rebecca added, "And we'll be here for him every step of the way. We won't let him go through this alone."

The car fell silent again as they drove through the streets of Oakland, lost in their own thoughts and worries. They knew that the road ahead would be long and difficult, but they were determined to see it through to the end.

***

The courtroom was filled with a perceivable tension on the second day of my trial. My lawyer, Jamal Jackson, arrived early to speak with me, I was looking more nervous than the previous day.

"Femi, you need to be calm today and trust me," Jamal said, placing a reassuring hand on my shoulder. "The prosecution will be bringing in some more witnesses, but we're prepared for this. We have a strong case."

I nodded, but my eyes were darting around the courtroom nervously. I couldn't help but feel like the odds were stacked against me.

As the judge entered the courtroom, everyone rose to their feet. The prosecutor called their first witness of the day, a former employee of mine at my tech startup. The witness claimed that I had made inappropriate advances towards her, and had even tried to kiss her.

Jamal's cross-examination was fierce, and he was able to establish that the witness had actually been fired from the company for underperforming, and that her claims were unsubstantiated.

As the prosecutor called the next witness, my heart sank as I heard the name Maria Guadalupe Fernandez. I couldn't believe my ears. I turned my head to look at Jamal, who sat next to me with a stern expression. My mind raced as Maria kept, with a stern expression on her face, made her way to the stand.

The courtroom erupted into whispers and murmurs, and my family sat in stunned silence. I tried to compose myself as I watched Maria take the oath and settle into the witness box. My mind was filled with questions. "How could Maria testify against me? Why would she do such a thing?"

The prosecutor began to ask Maria a series of questions, and I could feel the tension in the courtroom rise. I watched as Maria answered each question with a calm and collected demeanor. She described her relationship with me, how we had been together for several months, and how she had become pregnant with my child.

The prosecutor began questioning Maria, "Ms. Fernandez, can you describe for the court your relationship with the defendant?"

Maria hesitated before answering, "We were in a relationship. I loved him, and I believed he loved me too."

The prosecutor continued, "And when did you first experience Femi being violent with you?"

Maria took a deep breath before answering, "It was a few months into our relationship. He hit me during an argument."

The prosecutor pressed on, "And did this happen again?"

Maria nodded, tears streaming down her face, "Yes. It happened a few more times."

The prosecuting lawyer turned to the jury, "Ladies and gentlemen, victims of domestic violence often go back to their abusers. They believe their abusers will change, that they can fix things. But the truth is, the violence only escalates."

I sat there in shock, unable to believe that Maria was testifying against him. I wanted to stand up and scream, to tell her that I was sorry and that I loved her, but I knew it was too late.

Jamal could see the effect that Maria's testimony was having on me. He leaned over and whispered to me, "Stay calm, trust me."

The prosecutor continued, "Can you confirm that you are pregnant with Mr Femi Williams, child." The lawyer turned around to point to Femi. "The man sitting right there?"

"Yes, I am," Maria replied calmly.

"Did you tell Mr. Williams that you were pregnant with his child?" The lawyer pressed.

"No, I couldn't tell him." Maria answered.

The prosecuting lawyer leaned in, his voice low and steady, "You couldn't tell him? Why not?"

Maria looked down at her hands, wringing them in her lap. "I was afraid of what could happen," she repeated softly.

"Afraid? Of Femi?" The prosecutor's voice was incredulous, as if he couldn't believe what he was hearing.

Maria nodded, tears beginning to prick at the corners of her eyes. "Yes, I was afraid. He was always so angry, and he had a temper. I didn't know what he would do if I told him."

The prosecutor turned to the jury, his expression somber. "This is a common pattern with victims of domestic violence. They are too afraid to speak up, too afraid to leave. And when they do leave, they often return to their abusers. But that doesn't mean the abuse didn't happen."

He turned back to Maria. "Did Femi ever hurt you physically?"

Maria took a deep breath, trying to compose herself. "Yes," she said, her voice barely above a whisper. "He hit me. He pushed me. He threw things at me."

The prosecutor nodded, as if this was what he expected to hear. "And when did this happen?"

Maria thought back, her mind a jumbled mess of memories. "It happened several times over the course of our relationship. The last time was a few weeks before I found out I was pregnant."

The prosecutor nodded again, then leaned back on the prosecutor's table, his hands steepled in front of him. "Thank you, Ms. Fernandez. No further questions."

"We will take a quick fifteen minute break," the Judge announced.

The police guided me back to a holding cell with other people that potentially had their hearings that day.

As Maria stepped down from the witness stand, she felt a hand on her shoulder. She looked up to see Zeke, looking at her with assurance.

"Are you okay?" he asked, his voice gentle.

Maria shook her head, tears spilling down her cheeks. "I don't know," she said. "I just want this to be over."

Zeke nodded. "I know. We'll get through this, I promise."

As they made their way out of the courtroom, Maria felt like the weight of the world was on her shoulders. She didn't know how much more of this she could take.

***

The judge signaled for Jamal to start his cross-examination of Maria. Jamal stood up and faced Maria, his eyes locked with hers.

"Ms. Fernandez, can you tell me how you first met my client, Femi?" Jamal asked, his voice calm but stern.

Maria hesitated for a moment before answering, "I met him at a friend's party."

Jamal nodded and continued, "And what do you do for work, Ms. Fernandez?"

"I'm a nurse," Maria replied.

"Interesting," Jamal remarked. "So you must have a busy schedule then. Did you have time to see and spend time with my client?"

Maria looked down and whispered, "Yes."

Jamal leaned in and asked, "Were you in a committed relationship with my client, Mr Williams?" Jamal pointed to me.

Maria hesitated again before answering, "No."

Jamal nodded and asked, "So you were aware that my Femi Williams was seeing other women, since you were not in a committed relationship with him?"

Maria nodded silently.

The prosecuting lawyer objected, "Your Honor, this line of questioning is irrelevant to the case."

The judge nodded and said, "Sustained. Mr. Jackson, please focus on the case at hand."

Jamal nodded and asked, "Ms. Fernandez, did you ever see my client exhibit violent behavior towards you when you met him?"

Maria looked up and replied, "No."

Jamal took some steps towards the witness box and asked, "So when did Mr. Williams exhibit violent behavior towards you?"

Maria paused, "I don't remember from the top of my head," and answered.

"When was the last time he exhibited this violent behavior?" Jamal pressed.

"Some months into dating," Maria replied.

"Can you help me with what exactly happened," Jamal asked.

"Objection! The witness will have to live through the incident again," the prosecutor raised his voice.

"Objection overruled! Answer the question Ms. Fernandez," the judge said.

"I visited Femi, like I usually did for the weekend. We were lounging in his living room and we were watching a TV show. We didn't agree on a discussion, he held my wrist so hard, I screamed that he was hurting me and when he finally stopped I was bruised. He enjoys hurting me while having sex." Maria said.

Jamal nodded and asked, "Was that why you did not tell Mr. Williams that you were pregnant?"

Maria took a deep breath before answering, "I was afraid of what could happen. He had a temper, and I didn't want to make things worse."

Jamal nodded and walked towards his table to pick a disc and remote controller, the room was silent, you could hear a pin if it dropped before he hit play, focused on the TV screen and before continuing with his cross-examination.

"Please watch the screen, Ms Fernandez," Jamal said as he walked to the side of the jury, narrating what they were watching.

Maria's heart sank as Jamal played the video. She couldn't believe she was seeing herself at that moment. Her mind raced as she tried to come up with an explanation. She knew she had to think fast, or her entire testimony could be discredited.

Jamal paused the video, and Maria braced herself for his question. "Is that where you got the mark that you sent to the police?" he asked.

Maria hesitated for a moment before answering. "Yes," she finally said, her voice barely above a whisper.

Jamal turned to the jury, "But in the video, we clearly see that it was consensual," he said, his voice rising. "And yet, you claim that it was an act of violence."

The tension in the courtroom was touchable as Jamal continued to question Maria about her relationship with me. Maria tried to defend herself, but Jamal was relentless. He had clearly done his homework and was determined to discredit her testimony.

Jamal took a deep breath before addressing Maria again. "Let's talk about the text messages you showed to the police as evidence that Femi apologized for hurting you," he said.

Maria looked at him, her expression wavering. "Yes?" she replied, her voice barely above a whisper.

Jamal leaned in, his eyes fixed on Maria. "Can you tell us the date and time that you received those texts from Femi?" he asked.

Maria hesitated before answering. "It was on the night of August 12th," she said.

Jamal smiled sarcastically. "That's interesting, because according to the security footage from Femi's house, he was in his living room at that time with no phone in sight," he said.

Maria's eyes widened in shock, and the courtroom erupted in gasps and murmurs.

Jamal continued to play the video, pausing it again. "As you can see here, Femi was in his living room passed out from having consensual sex with you when that message was sent, he wasn't on his phone, he fell asleep on his couch," he said, pointing to the screen.

Maria's face turned pale, and she appeared to be struggling to compose herself.

"That's not possible," she said, her voice shaking. "I received those texts from Femi's phone."

Jamal raised an eyebrow. "Are you sure about that?" he asked. "Because according to our investigation, although those texts were sent from Femi's phone, you sent those messages to yours by yourself."

Maria's eyes widened in shock, and she looked as if she was about to faint. The courtroom was completely silent as Jamal continued to question her, his voice cool and collected.

The tension in the room was touchable as Jamal presented more evidence against Maria's testimony. The jury looked on intently, taking notes and whispering to each other. I sat in my seat, looking at Jamal with a mixture of gratitude and awe.

As the cross-examination continued, Maria began to feel more and more trapped. She knew that she had made a mistake by getting involved with Zeke, but she never expected it to go like this. It became clear that Maria's testimony was riddled with inconsistencies and lies.

The judge finally called for a recess, and Maria stumbled out of the courtroom, feeling humiliated and defeated. I hugged Jamal, thanking him for his help.

"I don't think we need Catherine's testimony anymore," Jamal whispered to me.

Despite the setback, the prosecutor was still confident that they had a strong case against me. But for my family and I, it felt like a small victory in a long and difficult battle.

The courtroom was silent as the judge asked for the closing statements from both lawyers. The prosecuting lawyer stood up, looking confident as he reiterated his earlier points. He reminded the jury of the evidence presented before them, how I had been violent towards Maria, and how I had refused to take responsibility for my actions.

Jamal Jackson stood up next, looking calm and collected. He reminded the jury of the inconsistencies in Maria's testimony and the evidence that showed she had sent herself the text messages from my phone. He emphasized that the burden of proof was on the prosecution, and they had not met that burden.

After the closing statements, the jury retired to deliberate on the verdict. The tension in the courtroom was observable as everyone waited anxiously for the verdict. My family held hands, my lawyer and also did the same, praying for a favorable outcome.

After what seemed like an eternity, the jury returned to the courtroom, and the leader announced the verdict. "We, the jury, find the defendant, Femi Williams, not guilty." The courtroom erupted in cheers as my family and I hugged each other, tears streaming down our faces.

Jamal smiled triumphantly as he shook my hand with a strong grip. The prosecuting lawyer looked stunned, unable to believe that he had lost the case. I hugged Jamal, and thanked him for believing in him. Jamal smiled and said, "I knew justice would prevail."

Meanwhile, Maria sat in shock as she realized the consequences of her false accusation. The judge sentenced her to two years in jail and community service for infringing on my privacy and falsely accusing me of a crime.

My family and friends left the courthouse with a sense of relief and gratitude that the truth had come out. I hugged my parents, and sister and thanked them for their unwavering support throughout the trial. I turned and it was Amaka reaching out her arms to hug me and said, "I'm so proud of you, Femi. You've been through so much, but you never gave up. You stood strong, and justice was served."

***

Outside the courthouse, reporters and cameras swarmed my family and I, eager to hear our reaction to the verdict. My parents, sister, and cousin Bidemi hugged me tightly as we spoke to reporters.

"Femi has always maintained his innocence, and we are grateful that the jury saw the truth," Bidemi said. "We are happy that justice has been served, and Femi can now move on with his life."

I thanked my lawyer, Jamal, for his hard work and dedication. "I am grateful for Jamal's tireless efforts in proving my innocence," I said. "I am also grateful to my family and friends for their support during this difficult time."

The trial may have ended, but the impact it had on my family and I would stay with us for a long time. We had come out victorious, but the scars of the trial would take time to heal.

***

After the trial, I felt a sense of relief wash over me. I couldn't believe I was finally free from the false accusations that had been made against me. I turned to Amaka, who had been by my side when the ordeal became public, and took her hand. "I couldn't have made it through this without you," I said, looking into her eyes.

Amaka smiled and squeezed my hand. "I'll always be here for you, Femi," she replied.

That night, I hosted a dinner party at my home in Oakland Hills, inviting all of my loved ones to celebrate my freedom. Amaka was there, along with Catherine, Bidemi, Rebecca, and even my parents.

As we sat around the dinner table, I couldn't help but feel grateful for the people in my life. We reminisced about old times and caught up on everything that had happened while I was going through the trial.

Catherine couldn't stop talking about how impressed she was with Jamal's defense strategy. Amaka was proud of me for staying strong throughout the trial, and Bidemi was grateful to have me back home.

As we ate dinner, they shared stories and laughed over inside jokes. I was grateful for the love and support of my family and friends. I realized that their support was what helped me get through the tough times, and I was glad to have them by my side.

***

With the trial now behind them, life seemed to return to a sense of normalcy for me and my loved ones. The summer months passed by quickly, with me spending and enjoying quality time with my family and friends.

During one of these summer days, I found myself sitting on the deck of my house in Oakland Hills, enjoying the warm breeze that swept across the hills. As I sipped my cold drink, I gazed out at the stunning view of the city below, feeling grateful for everything that I had.

Suddenly, I heard the sound of footsteps on the deck behind me, and I turned to see Amaka standing there, smiling at me. I felt his heart skip a beat at the sight of her, and I couldn't help but grin widely as I got up from my chair to greet her.

"Hey there," I said, pulling her in for a tight embrace.

"Hey yourself," Amaka replied, laughing as she hugged me back.

As we pulled away from each other, I looked at Amaka, taking in her beauty as if I was seeing her for the first time, there was an aura about her presence around me that I couldn't explain but the one thing that I realized was that at that moment, I knew that I wanted to spend the rest of his life with her.

"Amaka, there's something I need to tell you," I said, taking her hand in mine.

"What is it?" she asked, looking at me curiously.

"I love you," I said simply, looking deep into her eyes.

Amaka's eyes widened in surprise, and then a huge smile broke out on her face. "I love you too, Femi," she said, her voice filled with emotion.

In that moment, I knew that I had found my soulmate, and I knew that nothing would ever come between us. Together, we spent the rest of the day basking in our love and enjoying each other's company, knowing that we had found something truly special.

In the months that followed, Amaka and I relationship continued to blossom, and we found ourselves growing closer and closer with each passing day. We supported each other through the ups and downs of life, and we always knew that we could count on each other, no matter what.

Amaka was aware of my relationship with Catherine. It was hard for her, when she found out she didn't like the idea of sharing me with another woman but later realized that she would rather know and be friends with Catherine. She remembered that she was cordial, and very supportive during my trial and they got along when she didn't know, and now that she knows, she would rather be a friend than a competitor for my love, and attention.

Amaka and Catherine became friends, and did everything together, they went shopping, spa dates, running, movie nights and cooking for me.

And as for Maria, she eventually faced the consequences of her actions and was held accountable for her false accusations against me. She confessed to trying to paralyze me and how she got involved with Zeke to bring me down when I visited her in the correctional center she was being held at. I chose to forgive her and move on, knowing that I had found true happiness with Amaka by my side.

As Amaka and I settled into our new life together, my business began to thrive once again. With the help of my trusted team, I was able to restructure the company and fire the board of directors that had backed Zeke's unethical practices. I made sure that the company was now built on a foundation of integrity and transparency.

Meanwhile, Zeke was nowhere to be found. It was rumored that he had fled the country to avoid prosecution for his crimes, leaving behind a trail of ruined lives and shattered dreams. I was grateful that justice had finally been served, but I knew that there was still work to be done to ensure that FemCo continued to operate with integrity.

****

One day, I took Amaka on a surprise date to the Golden Gate Bridge. We walked along the bridge, enjoying the breathtaking view of San Francisco Bay. As we reached the middle of our trail, I pointed to a small plane flying across the bridge with a sign behind it saying, "Will you marry me?"

"That's cheesy," Amaka said laughing at herself, when she looked to her side, she saw that I had gotten down on one knee and pulled out a small velvet box.

"Amaka, I love you with all my heart, you are an awesome woman, you inspire me to be better with your nurturing and gentle spirit. No one deserves this version of me, only you" I said, my eyes glistening with tears. "Will you marry me?"

Amaka was speechless. Tears streamed down her face as she looked at me, feeling overwhelmed with emotion. She nodded her head yes, and I slipped a beautiful diamond ring on her finger.

We hugged and kissed as the sun set over the Golden Gate Bridge, and strangers passing by congratulated us. Amaka and I knew that we had a lot of work to do to build a strong and healthy relationship, but we were ready to face the challenges together.

As we drove back to the house, Amaka called her friends and family that would pick up her call that she was getting married, we discussed our future plans more granularly. We decided that we wanted to start a family and build a life together in Oakland Hills.

A few months later, Amaka and I got married in a beautiful ceremony surrounded by our friends and family. We exchanged our vows, promising to love, honor, and cherish each other for the rest of our lives.

After the wedding, Amaka and I went on a honeymoon to Hawaii, where we enjoyed our time together, basking in the warm sun and swimming in the crystal-clear waters.

As we returned home, Amaka and I were also excited to welcome a new member to their family. Maria had given birth to a baby girl while she was in prison and had decided to give me full custody of the child. Amaka and I were overjoyed at the prospect of being parents and we poured all our love into raising our new daughter.

Years later, my company continued to thrive, with me at the helm. I had built a reputation for myself as a fair and just businessman who always put my employees and customers first.

Amaka and I became a symbol of hope and inspiration for others who had gone through similar struggles. We now have children together and spoke publicly about our experiences and helped to raise awareness about domestic violence and false accusations.

Amaka and I love story had come full circle, and we knew that we had each other to thank for our happy ending.